Teaching
Broken Kids

Becoming a
Trauma-Informed
School

William N. Bender, Ph.D.

LEARNING®
SCIENCES
INTERNATIONAL

1641 Worthington Road, Suite 210, West Palm Beach, FL 33409
717.845.6300
email: pub@learningsciences.com
learningsciences.com

23 22 21 20 19   1 2 3 4 5

Publisher's Cataloging-in-Publication Data
provided by Five Rainbows Cataloging Services

Names: Bender, William, author.
Title: Teaching broken kids : becoming a trauma-informed school / William Bender.
Description: West Palm Beach, FL : Learning Sciences, 2019.
Identifiers: ISBN 978-1-943920-73-0 (paperback)
Subjects: LCSH: Affective education. | Social learning. | Child development. | Response to intervention (Learning disabled children) | Education--Social aspects. | Academic achievement. | BISAC: EDUCATION / Professional Development. | EDUCATION / Philosophy, Theory & Social Aspects. | EDUCATION / Non-Formal Education. | EDUCATION / Teaching Methods & Materials / General.
Classification: LCC LB1072.B46 2019 (print) | LCC LB1072.B46 (ebook) | DDC 370.15/34--dc23.

Table of Contents

Introduction

In the last several years, my wife Renet and I have dedicated ourselves to working, through our church, with a number of broken people, most of whom are young adults. The journey of understanding we were forced to take in order to do this work effectively is relevant, even in an instructional strategies book for public and private school teachers of all faiths. These individuals were deeply broken in that they have not experienced lives that have led to normal development, behaviorally, emotionally, or spiritually. Their brokenness may have resulted from early onset child abuse, child sexual abuse, neglect, and/or abject poverty and hunger. In some cases, these childhood challenges resulted in their participation in a variety of risky behaviors, such as early, frequent, and unprotected sex; recreational drug use; and, on occasion, drug or alcohol addiction. This, in turn, led to more brokenness as adolescents and young adults. We've learned that it makes little difference how these folks came to be broken; the only thing that really matters is the depth of their brokenness and their willingness to allow others to help them.

I should quickly explain that I use the term "broken" not in any pejorative or negative sense. In fact, I genuinely love and admire broken people. Perhaps now, near the end of my career in dealing with brokenness, I have become tired of the official labels. In my public school teaching years, I taught kids with more letters behind their name than the average MD; here's the list: ED, emotional disturbances; LD, learning disabilities; ADHD, attention deficit/hyperactivity disorders; ODD, oppositional defiant disorder; MR, mental retardation (today called *intellectual disabilities*). They have conduct/behavioral problems; they are victims of abuse of all types. They are often unwanted kids, homeless kids, and the list above doesn't even include "dual diagnosis" kids with the more expansive letter sets (e.g., LD/BD, ADHD/ED, ED/ODD).

1

At this point in my life, the word "brokenness" seems to fit these kids best. It is a summative term, and I believe a more positive term; after all, broken people, like broken things, can be fixed. Again, this term is certainly not intended as disrespect, nor is it intended to convey a harsh judgment of who these kids are (I believe the more clinical terms above do that). I just think of these kids and adolescents or young adults as kids who need help. My problem was that, in my public school teaching and throughout my career, I loved all these kids—at least, almost all of them. Perhaps I could see their struggles, or maybe I saw my own relatively minor issues in some of their major struggles. For whatever reason, this was enough to propel me to work with severely damaged people for more than 40 years. Today, a full decade after I left academia, I'm still writing books and doing workshops in this area, as well as working with a number of broken people in halfway houses, or simply folks I meet in church or elsewhere, as well as their kids. They are broken for all of the reasons presented above.

In the last several years, my wife and I have taught Sunday school classes for young adults who were broken (mostly recovering methamphetamine addicts and adult victims of childhood sexual abuse). We've also had a couple of recovering addicts move into our home as they completed accountability court requirements during an 18-month probation period. In addition, I've taught a Bible class for men at a halfway house recovery program over the last year, and Renet has tutored several of these young adults in mathematics as they struggled to earn their general education development (GED) degree—math is usually the subject that gives these folks difficulty. Finally, based on the Sunday school lessons I was writing for these folks, I recently completed a Christian curriculum book on that topic (*Bible Lessons for Broken People*; Covenant Books, 2019).

As you might imagine, we have personally spent scores of thousands of dollars assisting these individuals, as well as thousands and thousands of hours of time. We have been and are committed to this work, so much so that we established a foundation—The John Bender Foundation—to assist in this effort. That foundation pairs a grant of between $3,000 and $6,000, along with weekly "life coaching" from a Christian perspective, to these young adults to help them reestablish their lives. Usually these funds pay for a car for school attendance at the GED or two-year college level, or they may buy a computer to assist with their studies. The funds may be used for on-the-job work training or anything else that moves these young adults forward. You can read about some of these young adults, their challenges and their successes, on the foundation website (see https://www.thejohnbenderfoundation.org). Also, please do contact me directly if you would like to help with that effort.

Again, I mention that here to indicate the level of commitment my wife and I have made to these individuals. Simply put, we feel that this is some of the most important work we have ever done.

Now here's something that should surprise no one; many of these broken people have kids! As a second non-surprise, some of their children and adolescents are deeply broken emotionally, just like their parent or parents. As teachers, my wife and I have seen these broken kids sitting right there in the classroom, right beside children and adolescents with much more traditional, much more positive family backgrounds. Because you are reading this book for some reason, it's probably safe to assume you're a teacher and have seen these broken kids in your own classroom! You might want some ideas on how to deal with them. If so, this book should help.

Upon reflection, this means that there are really two groups of children and adolescents that may be broken—those raised by parents with negative childhood experiences and the children who, themselves, are undergoing horrible challenges in their family right now. Further, these two groups of kids tend to look very much alike in the classroom.

As you probably know, broken kids come from all races, all age groups, all religious groups, and all socio-economic groups, although there is somewhat more brokenness associated with impoverished homes in general. Still, brokenness happens across the spectrum, and as teachers, we must be vigilant in seeking ways to reach and teach these kids.

Of course, public school teachers should not approach these students from the perspective of personal religious beliefs. My wife and I had that option in much of the work described previously with young adults, but as public school teachers, a heavy religious emphasis will not usually be an option. However, teachers do have a moral obligation to make every effort possible to reach these students—many of whom seem to have completely shut out the entire world—in some way and teach them what they need to know to succeed in life and thus escape their brokenness.

The first chapter of this book provides information on what I've discovered about broken people in general, with a later focus on my observations of these broken kids. Although I've written a number of books on classroom discipline for teachers over the years and have personally taught adolescents with special needs for a number of years prior to teaching in higher education, my experiences for this book also include providing child care on a 24/7 basis for three different families from the broken people described previously. In some cases, when parents' work schedules didn't articulate well, or when assisting single parents, my wife and I have hosted these kids in our home for anywhere between 24 and 72 hours straight. I am retired, and I could help some of these folks in that fashion with 24/7 childcare for three days in a row. Thus, even while I entered my "social security years," I've been changing diapers, planning play dates, and taking these kids to the park, or to the pool, or swimming in the local creek. At this point, I've all but memorized *Moana, Coco, Word Party, Sing,* and most of *Little Baby Bum!* The mothers out there will understand each of those titles!

With this set of very recent experiences, I can honestly say that I now know broken kids about as well as I know broken people. So, this book is a book for teachers who, in either religious or non-religious teaching situations, have to reach and teach these broken kids. If you can acquire these specialized skills and begin to employ some of these specialized strategies, you will reach these kids in a way that most teachers cannot. Further, you will find this work to be more rewarding than virtually anything you've done previously—at least, we did.

It is my sincere hope that this book can assist in that regard.

CHAPTER 1

Warriors

A Way to View Brokenness

I realize that beginning a book on instructional strategies for public schools with a report on my Christian growth in this area is a bit unorthodox, and this introduction and chapter 1 are the only sections in this book written from an overtly Christian perspective. However, because I believe that this book is more easily understandable in that context, I present these here. Chapter 1 comes from a Sunday school lesson book I've done, and it tells of my growing understanding of so many troubled kids and young adults today. Even these two book sections are understandable and useful to those of all faiths.

The remainder of this book beyond chapter 1 was not written with any religious emphasis.

In late January 2017, I went rogue. I created a Sunday school class in the balcony of our church; it was the only empty space I knew of on Sunday morning. I did that with no permission whatsoever, because I felt I had to.

The plain fact is, our church was filled with hundreds of Christians who had been steeped in Christianity all their lives. Most came from good families—these were and are some of the best people I know. However, our church had nothing to offer folks whose lives were truly broken. We had no specific Sunday school class for folks who have already lived in hell. Of course, Jesus was there in that church, and Almighty God was worshiped there, but we still didn't have the class that these broken folks needed.

Several of these broken folks were raised in hell, and I had five deeply broken people, ranging in age from 18 up to 36, coming the very next Sunday! I'd invited them to come, so I had some serious responsibility there. Officially creating a new Sunday school class (I feared) had to go through time-consuming committees, etc. I needed an appropriate class for these guys in four days!

So I went rogue. I needed a quick Bible-based lesson on feeling harshly judged when one was going to church. This was one of their biggest concerns. They'd all told me they would probably feel judged if they even went near a church! I needed a lesson on that topic. I needed one on why church attendance was worth it, and another class on dealing with overwhelming, paralyzing guilt. What's worse, I needed those lessons right then! So I talked with my wife, and we prayed. God seemed to be saying, "Just do it! You can apologize later!" So I did.

I created those lessons, and I taught them to my five guests, these broken people, over the next three weeks. After that, I went to my pastor, a man I deeply respect, and confessed to going rogue. I apologized and explained why I'd done it. I promised to never do it again. He then smiled and said, "I saw you guys up in that sanctuary balcony during Sunday school time. I started to go up, but I figured something important might have been going on. I guess it was. Okay, so now I think we've got a new Sunday school class." May God be praised for that man, for his decision, and for all that has come out of that!

During that rogue period, I wrote down a few thoughts, presented below, about and for those broken people (Bender, 2018). This text was never intended to be a Sunday school lesson, much less a section for educators. In fact, I was not sure I would ever show it to anyone when I wrote it. Still, I eventually did, and I've found that this was the best place to begin with broken people, or at least broken young adults. It will also help understand broken kids, so I decided to present it here. It may explain a few harsh truths about broken people of any age that will help teachers, will help anyone, deal with them more effectively.

Since I wrote this, a number of broken people have said this is important stuff, so take as long as you like with this. Maybe it can open up your thoughts a bit on how to view broken people.

Thoughts on Broken People, from a Long, Sleepless Night

So this happened at 4:34 a.m. on February 2, 2017 (Bender, 2018). We'd begun to meet in the church balcony on Sunday morning—three women and two men, broken people from the school of hard knocks! They each knew hell; knew it intimately. They were broken, just like me. Reflecting on what we might call ourselves (and having rejected "The Balcony Bunch"), I began to think of who they are, or who we are. As you can see, that led to an absolute seizure of writing. These are my notes to them, and to you, and certainly to myself, which is why verb tense and pronouns change so often. (Please pardon the stream of consciousness here.). I hope some of this helps, but why in all that is holy did this have to happen at 4:34 in the morning?

I began to think of common traits, if any, that victims of abuse and/or addiction might share, but there's the first problem: I hate the terms *victims of abuse* and *victims of addiction*. The folks I have come to know are anything but victims. They may have made a few bad choices, or maybe even many bad choices, but they are not victims. I don't like the term *survivors* either; they are living and moving on with life—doing much more than just surviving. Even though many of their attitudes and self-perceptions are predicated on having suffered abuse or gone through years of addiction, their past history of abuse does not define them. These folks are much more than victims or survivors. They have seen the enemy, and they looked into the pit of hell; some lived there. Some were born there. They know the depths of total depression and absolute despair. They've looked into the eyes of darkness; of evil incarnate; and the amazing truth is that they've survived! At the very least, they were not destroyed. Most are struggling with their personal demons still, and they know they always will. Still, they are here and moving on with life. That alone is a miracle for many of them.

They have many scars, but they came through alive. They remind me of the Knights Templar of old—warrior brothers who fought, bled, fell, and got up again and again. They survived with their many battle scars. The scars are different for each one, but all have them. I have a few myself, but nothing like these guys. They are braver than I'll ever be. These men and women are pure warriors—the best term I can come up with. This is going to be fun; may God help us in this, and I surely hope I don't screw this up!

Despite having gone through the worst abuse imaginable (at least some of them), there is a spark of hope here, a fierce pride, some type of light deep in their soul, even in the darkest depths of despair. If they have seen evil up close, they have also seen something else.

Be Still, and Know that I Am God!

The last thing this group wants is pity. Clearly, there is something to build on here, and that is why most of them are succeeding; most are moving forward in life. Those that aren't were not invited to come with us up here to the balcony. My thoughts and prayers for those several that I chose not to invite to join us. Some folks just didn't seem to be ready, and I made the call on whom to invite. It was mine alone. May a merciful, loving, benevolent God forgive me if I was wrong in even one instance!

So what does define them? Who are they as a group? Although all their situations are different and each individual is different, are there common issues here, common traits? I'm usually pretty good at seeing who people really are, and I've studied psychology, personality, character traits, temperament, and an array of mental health problems for decades. Still, with these individuals, I didn't feel that I'd gotten a full and complete handle on it. That's probably why I'm writing this—to clarify some thoughts.

These guys often surprised me, and for a simple mind like mine, they fit into no clear category. Still, I thought I saw some things that most of them—but certainly not all—have in common. So here are the thoughts, for whatever they may be worth.

First, these guys in general begin to believe their abusers in a deep sense. They begin early on to think that the verbal abuse or physical abuse they went through tells them who they really are—that's Stockholm syndrome at its finest. The physical and emotional abuse they endured is deeply internalized, and they somehow think they might have deserved it. This is the darkness inside them; a blackness that covers their life, their joy. They feel unworthy. They even identify with their abusers and often want to "forgive" them. They believe that if anybody really knew them deep down, they couldn't possibly love them. They believe on some level that they are unworthy of love and of happiness. This has led to suicide attempts for most of them, though not all.

This interior darkness leads to horrid life decisions. For example, in most future relationships, broken people will never give of themselves fully; they never open up. Further, they will almost always choose other abusers in future relationships, and thus continue the pattern, to affirm who they believe they are—an unlikable, unlovable, unworthy person. That only stops when they intentionally, through strength, integrity, spiritual development, maturity, and self-knowledge (as well as great effort), break that pattern. Some make that journey successfully, whereas others do not.

Because they do internalize their past history of abuse and tend to believe deeply in their own worthlessness, many of them get really, really pissed off. They are angry, viciously angry, at the world in general, and that transfers to almost anyone they come into contact with. When they point that harsh light of anger and rage at you, you should run! Run far and fast, and stay gone for a while. Just let them win that battle. If you are wise, you will come back, and when you come back, you will be quite humbled. That's the only way back in with these guys—being humble—and even then, you won't get very far in.

I have come to see that the anger comes from some spark, some faded light of hope within them, some sense that they are not who their abusers have told them they are. That spark is their pride—the good side of pride, pride that helps one survive the harshest circumstances. Pride can help one survive hell. Maybe that kind of pride is God's small voice on the inside; Jesus speaking, if you will.

It is their pride reaching out and trying to survive. There seems to be an ongoing, constant battle inside them—they believe they deserved the abuse, yet on another level they know they didn't, that they are much more worthy than that. This internal battle keeps these guys emotionally exhausted, and some show continual rage.

They see others as clueless to their internal struggles. In general, they are right. Thus, beyond general, meaningless, shallow conversation, most others are unworthy of their time. That is why most "Bible bangers" fail to reach these broken people. Energetic religious folks, steeped in Christian teachings for their entire lives, may very well be "on fire for God" but in general, most simply don't understand this total brokenness very well. You can't just "save" someone existing in a parallel universe. A hearty handshake and a Biblically based smile—what I call the "Great Christian Grin"—leaves these folks cold. A Baptist with a five-minute testimony, or a couple of Jehovah's Witnesses with a smile and a Bible at the door, can't touch these guys.

I'm not saying here that testimonies or bibles passed out at the door don't change lives—they often do. I'm just saying that for this batch of very broken people, much more will be needed. You have to get real with them; you have to talk to them and really listen to them. You need to hear what they say as well as everything they *don't* say. You should tell them your failures once in a while so they know they are not alone in failure. You should even be willing to get dirty with them, getting into their problems and worries. Drive them to their court dates. Ask questions. Learn of their felonies and misdemeanors. Learn the lingo. Most of all, use their language, including all the words not usually heard in church or school. Make just a bit of an opening using their language, and you can sometimes reach them. Then, God will step in! Jesus will use the smallest open door to touch their soul. He'll worry about their language (and yours) later.

Some of these broken folks had "partners" in and during their abuse—siblings or maybe cousins who suffered the same abuse with them. I've seen that once or twice before. Those partners become soul-mates, bonded together through unimaginable horrors, like men in battle. As with men or women in war, those partners provide strength to each other and they are deeply bonded for life. No one else will ever touch—no one else will ever come close—to the depth of that relationship, and no one should try. Those partners provide a strength to and for each other more profound than death itself—brighter than the sun. There is great strength there, but you as an outsider will never control that strength. They won't share control of that bond, nor should they. It is theirs alone. Do watch that bond carefully, and when private communion begins between the partners, know enough to shut up and get the hell out of the way. Important stuff, good stuff, even great stuff, can and does happen at that point, even with no guidance from you.

Broken people will not trust you unless you earn their trust through unimaginable time and effort. Few make that effort; fewer still have the time.

You will never earn their trust. They really don't trust. Suck it up and live with it. Not everything has to make sense. It's really not about you.

You will never earn their trust, so don't try. Of course, you should always, always, always try. What are you here for, if not to try? What am I here for, if not to try?

Broken people sometimes relate together quite normally. They can and do, on occasion, relate to others normally. For them it is a "show" or pretense, but let's get real for a minute. Maybe a certain pretense is the basis of most social interaction for all of us. When we casually ask someone "How are you today?" do we ever really care? To broken people, those communications are merely phoniness.

Broken people quickly ascertain whether you are "of" them or not.

When they run you off, you should come back. You should always come back. Generally, they are okay with it and if not, trust me, they will let you know. Go away at that point, but come back. Always, always, always come back.

They judge, often harshly, sometimes cruelly, but usually quite accurately. They have a great, built-in BS detector and zero tolerance for phony relationships. They can smell a phony person from across the room. If that harsh, cruel judgment falls on you, run for your life.

They do not, not ever, respect a phony.

We (those of us whom they perceive as non-broken people) are all phony. We are presumed to be phony unless we are one of them.

We will never, ever be one of them.

They lie. They tend to lie somewhat less than the average Joe, but they do lie.

Broken people never ask for help. Even when they know they should, and truly believe they will get it, they don't ask. When they need it, they never ask for help. When they want it, they never ask for help. When they know help is available, that someone really wants to help, they never ask for help. Asking for help, in their mind, causes them to lose control of part of their lives, and they can never lose control. So here's some big damn news: *They never ask for help!*

Asking for help actually hurts these guys. When fierce pride is all you have, then that fierce pride is what you cling to. That is the dark side of pride—it holds help far away. So they never ask for help! Now I realize how very stupid I've been on that score in hoping that they would begin to ask for help. Then again, I've been stupid before. This batch ain't my first rodeo and these guys won't be my last. I'll find another batch of misfit warriors, and I'll be stupid again. I'll make many of the same mistakes again, trust me!

Some of them, on the rarest of occasions, ask for help. Didn't I mention surprises before?

Sometimes, I think of these guys as the walking dead, emotional eunuchs that can't possibly survive. They show no emotion; they share nothing. They celebrate no achievements at all! Pride—the dark pride, can mean indifference even to positive things in life. How in hell are these guys succeeding at all?

They have to have control—they are all control freaks! If they cannot have some control over a given situation, they leave! They just get out.

Sometimes, they look like they can't love, that they can't feel. Those emotional walls helped to protect them and they still protect them. The walls protected their core, their deeper self, during their sojourn in hell. The fact is that they feel love deeply. They are overly sensitive to any criticism because they feel everything deeply. That is why they withdraw from the world—some of them actually hibernate emotionally, almost never leaving their home (I had one of those up in the balcony)! Of course, they desire most of all acceptance, and even respect, but certainly not pity.

11

Broken people know they have worth, and they know they have more wisdom in their little toe than most of us acquire in a lifetime. They have lived in hell, and most of us haven't. That's why the rest of us seem clueless. We aren't dumb—they don't see us as dumb—just clueless.

They don't communicate with those of us deemed unworthy of their time. In fact, none of us are deemed worthy of their time.

They never apologize, not ever. Even when they know they should. It is a sign of weakness. Their dark pride means they can show no weakness!

They really are seeking growth, seeking God, or seeking something meaningful in life. They want something greater than the pain, or greater than what they have felt before. They want things to be fair and to make sense. They want a good life, a reason to exist. That is why some of them—the female warriors—have babies. They create someone to love. That is why others tend to seek relationships, most of which will fail, because of their emotional self-protective walls. If you won't or can't give yourself completely to someone else, should you pretend to give yourself at all? These guys try and try again in relationships that are doomed based on their inability to open up.

That deeply hidden desire to be open to others is the key, if there is a key. There is room here for emotional growth and even spiritual growth and, perhaps, even for the Spirit of God. Some broken folks know God and some don't, but all are seeking.

I really hope I don't screw this up; much can be accomplished here, if I don't screw this up.

They are all stronger than me. They are stronger than most folks I know. They are warriors—I seem to keep coming back to that. I don't know if that's the name we need or not; it may be a bit too militaristic for some. Ultimately, they will decide on their name. The world, the universe, owes them at least that.

What I do know is that the broken people have a story to tell, probably more than one. They have much to teach us—we who are clueless to what adversity really is.

So now it's 6:52 a.m., and Wifey sets her alarm for 7. My day begins; our pawed friends go out, and I turn the coffee on. Time for me to get my sorry self up and take The Lady her coffee while she's still in bed—she deserves it. She is nonverbal for a while when she gets up, but when I've done my job right and delivered the java, her first guttural grunt in the morning usually means something like, "Good morning, and thanks for the coffee!"

I'm not sure if writing this was worth it, but maybe it was—who knows? Maybe I'll share this with you guys up in the balcony. If I do, then I hope it makes sense or might make you think a bit. Please don't take anything to heart here, unless you think it fits. I can be wrong, and many times I am, at least as often as I'm right. If you like, mark this up and give it back to me. Tell me if a paragraph really spoke to you, if it is on the money. Then, put a big BS beside the sections that are just plain wrong, but do tell me why. Please explain, if you can. I do want to understand. Maybe some of this even made you smile.

I should have phoned every one of you jokers at 4:34 a.m. just to make your phone ring that early! Do you see the crap you guys put me through?

Anyway, I love you guys, every single one of you sorry, broken guys.

I'll see you next Sunday up in the balcony. I'm looking forward to it.

Final Note from the Original Text

The final name of our group, "Rogue Warriors," was selected by the group in late February 2017, after I shared this document with them (Bender, 2018). Some were already Christians; one or two were not. Two of these broken folks had kids. They quickly became my friends, my personal band of rogues, and they were certainly all warriors in every sense. They've made it through hells that few of us will ever know. They've earned the honor of that title, and so much more. These guys really are the bravest folks I know. They are my personal superheroes. May God smile on our upcoming discussions and our joint battles.

Note to Teachers

Again, the document above was written in a Christian context that, I hope, provided some basis for the rest of the book. I realize that many readers of this book, a book intended for all teachers, may hold other religious beliefs or none at all, and while I debated not using this first chapter or editing it in some fashion, I decided to leave it as is for the most part, because it has proved very helpful in opening doors with young adults. Some version of this might even be shared with broken adolescents, if you choose.

When considering how teachers should approach broken kids in the classroom, understanding some of the above might help teachers view those challenged and highly emotional or enraged kids is a slightly different way. These kids may appear as angry, enraged, and violent on the surface, but deep down they are broken. If we can see them that way, we just might be more able to reach them. At any rate, that is my hope.

CHAPTER 2
Broken Kids

Kids Living in Hell

The Question on Causal Factors

Many kids in schools today live in hell. They have been repeatedly traumatized in a variety of ways, and as a result, they just seem to be broken. As discussed in the previous chapter, such behavioral and emotional malfunctioning most frequently stems from home environments that resemble hell much more closely than they resemble loving families. These home environments are typically dominated by fear, harsh language, abject poverty, intentional cruelty, neglect, or child abuse—either physical or emotional. As teachers, most of us have experienced the child or adolescent whom we could never seem to reach, the one who was always mad, fighting, shouting, or simply completely withdrawn from the world. Veteran teachers can spot broken kids within 20 minutes on the first day of school based only on their classroom behaviors.

Whereas some of those behaviors may be subtle, others are anything but! The broken kid might be an enraged second-grade boy who finds, or more accurately seeks out, the very first opportunity to fight with someone in the class. For that kid, fighting is often territorial—he is staking out a territory for his own safety and letting others know not to mess with him! He believes he is establishing control of his world and thus protecting himself with such enraged and violent behavior. Further, his perspective may be right, in his world. He may come from a home environment in which such preemptive violence, or self-protective violence, works!

Teachers might have noticed the fourth-grade girl with scraggly, unkept hair, who dresses way too provocatively and never seems to engage meaningfully with any adult. That is a young girl for whom human interaction holds danger, and in her home that might, in fact, be the case. Another broken child might be the adolescent who seems to mumble only one-syllable responses, and seems to withdraw within themselves when any adult comes close. Many, if not most, of these broken kids won't look any adult in the eye.

Some broken kids are overly dependent on their parents for protective help in difficult situations. If the danger in their home background comes from a father, for example, the mother may be overprotective to the point at which her "Help" may be destructive of the child's or adolescent's ability to manage challenges in their own world. These kids are usually upper elementary age or older, and they might get their Moms to contact their teachers whenever homework is not done or when they fail an exam. Moms who are overwhelmed with guilt will often fight their children's battles for them, and over the long-term this overprotection can do more damage than other forms of abuse.

Of course, these are only potential reasons for various kid's behaviors, and we must be aware that there are many possible reasons for childhood misbehaviors other than brokenness. In one sense, almost all kids misbehave some, and only a small percentage of kids—maybe 15% or 20%—are truly broken. However, if we as teachers see only the behavior problem and concern ourselves only with the classroom disruption the problem brings,

> *Of course, while there are many potential reasons for brokenness, we must be aware that there are many possible reasons for childhood misbehaviors other than brokenness.*

we might miss seeing the fundamental brokenness of some misbehaving children and adolescents. Personally, I've realized I'm a much better and much more in-touch teacher if I look for why kids might do whatever it is they do. I can then, sometimes, spot the brokenness and make a few inquiries about it.

Now, it should be obvious that if parents were essentially raised in hell, it is not unreasonable to suspect that the home they will eventually create for their own kids will have some elements of hell in it. Again, almost all kids in school misbehave some, and some do it on a fairly frequent basis. Thus, in teasing out these kids from challenged backgrounds, it helps to ask several questions like, "How many troubled, truly broken kids are there? How many kids live in hell? Who are they? How will I, as a teacher, know them?"

Unfortunately, we don't really know the ultimate answers to these questions, but we can look at some related data. Of course, when these questions are asked in a professional context, they are phrased a bit differently. One might ask, for example, any of the following:

How many kids now live in poverty?

How many kids go hungry at times?

How many kids are abused by family members?

How many kids are sexually abused?

How many kids experience deep clinical depression?

How many kids demonstrate suicidal ideation or attempt suicide?

What are the presenting indicators of these types of home-based challenges?

More Complex Factors

Although the questions above can give professional educators a starting place, none of the usual questions really focuses on the answers we need. For example, simply knowing the poverty rate and the percentages of abused children doesn't really summarize the reality for these kids; a statistic on poverty is not the same as a gnawing hunger in one's gut. Further, any and all of the life challenges in the questions above probably create deep, abiding emotional scars, which may be manifested differently for different kids. In short, the same life challenge will manifest differently in the behavior of different kids.

Next, these factors often overlap, and any one of the threats to development noted above can interact with and influence other negative factors in a kid's life. Finally, none of these questions really tease out the specifics on how many kids are raised by severely broken people. We simply don't know how a parent's brokenness impacts a kid's brokenness. Of course, most educators suspect that parents' life disruptions do negatively impact kids, but it is at least possible that some broken parents raise reasonably normal kids, particularly if there is a mitigating influence toward normalcy in the child's life—a next-door relative or neighbor, a minister or rabbi, or a coach that might serve as a more stable role model for the child than the parent or guardian at home.

Even if we had all of these answers, that would merely move us to the next set of increasingly complex questions.

What do these broken kids look like in the classroom?

How do they behave?

How do they differ from kids with more "typical" behavioral problems?

What do we do with these kids in class once we verify a significant brokenness?

Is long-term therapy the only option for all broken kids?

How do we teach kids who are receiving such therapy?

How can I reach these kids in my classroom in some meaningful way?

Getting a Handle on Brokenness

While questions abound, one fundamental truth applies to all broken kids—they have been repeatedly exposed to a wide variety of childhood traumas of one form or another. Thus, perhaps the best way to get a handle on broken children is transformation of the teacher's question when confronted by an outrageous misbehavior in the classroom. When a child shouts curses at the teacher in class or explodes into violence, the teacher might normally think, "What's wrong with you?" If we, as professionals, can transform our perspective to ask a different question, "What's happened to you?" we can get a much richer perspective on broken kids (Adams & Dorado, 2013).

Therefore, we'll begin with what we do know about childhood traumas, the causal factors that cause brokenness. These include childhood poverty, abuse, and other insults that can disrupt lives of these children. Then we'll move to the more complex questions about specific behavioral manifestations in the classroom. Finally, all subsequent chapters of this book will identify and describe strategies for these broken kids and suggest specific strategies for various types of brokenness.

Risk Factors Associated with Brokenness

The litany of risk factors associated with brokenness is seemingly endless, and while not all of these can be described herein, a brief discussion of the more important risk factors is warranted. In fact, these risk factors very often overlap, and in many cases, the signs that children are experiencing something that can lead to brokenness are very similar. Having a sense of what these major risk factors are can help teachers understand what to consider when dealing with broken kids. At a minimum, factors such as poverty, hunger, addicted parents, child abuse, and suicidal ideation must be considered critical when discussing risk factors that lead to brokenness (Bellum, 2012; Rind, Tromovitch, & Bauserman, 1998; Whealin & Barnett, 2007).

Kids Living in Poverty

Data from the 2016 US Census suggest that 40 million Americans live in poverty, but that number changes from year to year as economic recessions come and go. Further, according to the 1959 US Census Bureau data, 40 million Americans lived in poverty—just like today! Clearly, the US population grew between 1959 and 2016, so simply using the overall number of persons in poverty can be misleading. In fact, the overall number has ranged between a low of 25 million in 1974 to a high of 47 million in 2013.

A more accurate measure of poverty is based on the percentage of the total population living in poverty. In 1959, 22% of Americans in poverty, whereas today between 12% and 14% do so based on 2016 census data. This documents a downward overall trend in poverty. Still, all experts agree that childhood poverty continues to be a significant problem in the US. For example, in addition to those living below the poverty line, nearly 33% of Americans live in families that are only slightly above the poverty line. Some experts use the phrase "near poverty" to discuss that population group. Further, poverty varies from state to state, with the highest poverty rates in Kentucky, Alabama, New Mexico, Mississippi, and Louisiana (ranging from 19% to 22%). Data also show that poverty rates are persistently higher in some rural areas and in many inner-city areas than in other parts of the country.

Between 12% and 14% of children today live in poverty, and 2.8 million kids live in extreme poverty.

Some population specialists also use the term "extreme poverty" when discussing poverty in the US. Extreme poverty may be defined as households living on less than $2 per day, excluding government benefits. Currently, 1.5 million households in the US, homes that include some 2.8 million children, live in extreme poverty. As one might imagine, these are the homes most closely associated with broken kids, but poverty often overlaps with various other problems such as childhood hunger or addicted parents.

Childhood Hunger

Childhood hunger and poverty very often go hand in hand, and while there is no one indicator of childhood hunger, federal definitions do discuss the concept of "food insecurity." Households with "low food security" are homes where availability of food at mealtime was not assured at least once within the previous 12 months, but in these homes, children did not directly experience hunger long-term. Homes with "very low food security" were homes in which receiving a meal or any food at all was not a certainty and children did experience hunger at some point. Census records indicate that about 6.5 million children, or 8.8% of all children, lived in households that were considered to be "food insecure" at one level or another in 2016.

Other non-government data, however, indicate an even more troubling picture. A report from the Annie E. Casey Foundation (2018) indicated that 14 million children (or 19% of all kids nationwide) go to bed or to school hungry on occasion. In that report, childhood hunger was shown to be highest in Louisiana and New Mexico, where 28% of children lived in food insecure homes.

Child Abuse and Neglect

Data from the Children's Bureau of the US government indicated that in 2015 one in every 100 children suffered some form of child abuse or neglect. *Abuse* is often understood as any form of inappropriate touching, beating, or physical punishment which harms or injures a child or adolescent. *Neglect* is defined as the failure of the parent or guardian to provide for the child's basic needs, including medical, educational, physical, or emotional needs. Seventy-five percent of children in this category suffer from neglect, without any physical abuse. The other 25% suffer from physical or sexual abuse, coupled with neglect.

However, there is some good news herein. According to a report from the Crimes Against Children Research Center in 2012, there is increasing evidence that the incidence of child abuse has decreased in the last two decades, as society has become more aware of the issue. According to that report, there has been a 56% decline in physical abuse and a 62% decline in sexual abuse between 1992 and 2010.

One in 100 children suffer from abuse or neglect, and of those, 75% suffer from neglect only without experiencing physical or sexual abuse.

No group of children is immune from child abuse or neglect. Abuse and neglect occur in all racial, socio-economic, and ethnic groups. Further, abuse and neglect know no age boundaries; data show that 27% of abused or neglected children are three years of age or younger. However, data also show that poverty does play a role in abuse. Children in poor families are three times as likely to be abused and seven times as likely to be neglected as other kids. Also, children in one-parent homes and children whose parents are unemployed are at greater risk for abuse and neglect. Awareness of these problems has increased drastically in recent years, and most teachers have been well prepared with information of the various indicators of these problems, as well as instructions on what to do if abuse or neglect is suspected.

Childhood Sexual Abuse

In contrast, childhood sexual abuse is less well recognized. Childhood sexual abuse is a form of child abuse in which an adult or older adolescent uses a minor for sexual stimulation or exploitation, and it may include such things as direct sexual activities, indecent exposure, or using a child to produce pornography. Although both sexes can be victims of childhood sexual abuse, girls are more likely to be victimized than are boys. In the US, approximately 14.5% of women and 7.2% of men were sexually abused when they were children (Gorey & Leslie, 1997; Rind et al., 1998; Whealin & Barnett, 2007).

However, many experts suspect that the stigma associated with such abuse leads to underreporting this problem, and this may suggest that these figures should be much higher. Even though studies differ on the relative rates of childhood sexual abuse in different races, it is clear that this phenomenon, like other forms of abuse and neglect, occurs in all races and ethnic groups.

Of all the risk factors that are associated with brokenness, this factor seems to be one of the most devastating for children, particularly if the abuse is ongoing or takes place over a long period of time. Effects of childhood sexual abuse may be manifested immediately or many years after the abuse has ended, and they include a litany of problems such as anxiety disorders, eating disorders, post-traumatic stress disorder, long-term clinical depression, stress-related physical symptoms, increased involvement with the justice system, increased medical problems in adulthood, and even suicide. Clearly, when one considers factors that lead to severe brokenness, childhood sexual abuse is one of the most important. Box 2.1 presents several websites that can provide more information on childhood sexual abuse and specifically what teachers should be looking for.

Box 2.1
Information on Childhood Sexual Abuse

The following websites provide additional information on childhood sexual abuse:

Child Matters—Indicators of child sexual abuse

www.childmatters.org.nz/85/learn-about-child-abuse/recognise-the-signs
    /sexual-abuse

South Eastern CASA—Behavioural indicators of child sexual abuse

https://www.secasa.com.au/pages/indicators-of-child-sexual-abuse/

National Society for the Prevention of Cruelty to Children (UK):
    Sexual abuse—Signs, indicators and effects

https://www.nspcc.org.uk/preventing-abuse/child-abuse-and-neglect
    /child-sexual-abuse/signs-symptoms-effects/

Personally, having worked with a number of broken adults over the years who experienced long-term childhood sexual abuse, I can attest that some of the most difficult persons to reach include both men and women who were victims. When this factor is present in one's brokenness, trust will be even more of a critical issue than for children and young adults who experienced other risk factors. Thus, with society somewhat less aware of this problem than for other forms of abuse, and given the underreporting of this phenomenon and the devastating long-term damage resulting from childhood sexual abuse, teachers must assume a more aggressive search for victims of this form of abuse.

When seeing the same children in one's class daily, teachers quickly form opinions on who the kids are, and as we learn our students' personalities and personal quirks better, we may not see each child with "fresh eyes" on a daily basis. This is how childhood sexual abuse can "slip in" beneath the radar. Teachers may miss subtle changes in their students' behaviors, such as a normally boisterous boy becoming consistently quiet or suddenly becoming aggressive, or a young girl suddenly wearing excessive makeup or provocative clothing. Of course, sometimes kids do get quiet suddenly, or become aggressive, or begin to mimic makeup or clothing habits of adults in the household. In fact, most changes such as these do not indicate onset of either abuse or childhood sexual abuse. Still, teachers should trust their intuition as well as their knowledge of their students, and ask questions if such sudden changes occur. Further, all teachers should remain vigilantly observant of all students in the class. On occasion, sudden changes such as these might indicate some difficulty at home. Box 2.2 lists a number of other indicators of potential child sexual abuse.

Addicted Parents as a Risk Factor

Research shows that 25% of children in America grow up in households where substance abuse is present, and children who grow up in such households are more than twice as likely to develop addictions themselves, either as adolescents or young adults (American Addiction Centers, 2018; Bellum, 2012). Further, such children demonstrate an array of behavioral problems including poor academic performance, conduct disorders in school, emotional or social behavioral problems, lower self-esteem, increased anxiety or depression, and increased manifestations of risky behaviors such as early sexual encounters or early experimentation with illegal drugs.

Twenty-five percent of children grow up in households where substance abuse is present, and those children are more than twice as likely to develop addictions themselves.

Box 2.2
Indicators of Childhood Sexual Abuse

- A child reporting sexual abuse in a disguised way (e.g., "I know a girl who . . .")
- Persistent and inappropriate sexual play with peers, toys, animals, or themselves
- A girl inserting objects in her vagina or sexually aggressive behavior with others
- "Humping" toys in sexual positions
- Detailed and overly sophisticated understanding of sexual behavior
- Sexual themes in the child's artwork, stories, or play
- Fear of going home, or expressing a desire to live in a foster home or institution
- Regressive behavior (e.g., excessive clinginess or the sudden onset of behavior problems)
- Soiling and wetting when these were not formerly a problem
- A child appearing disconnected or focused on fantasy worlds
- Sleep disturbances and nightmares
- Marked changes in appetite
- Fear states (e.g., anxiety, depression, phobias, obsession)
- Overly compliant behavior, as often young people who have been abused have experienced extensive grooming behaviors
- Delinquent or aggressive behavior
- Increased inability to concentrate in school and/or sudden deterioration in school performance
- Truancy/running away from home
- Excessively seductive behavior and/or sexual activity
- Drug/alcohol abuse
- Prostitution (There is a strong correlation between child sexual abuse and teenage prostitution.)
- Self-mutilation (i.e., cutting of arms, legs; burning; homemade tattoos)
- Suicidal feelings and suicide attempts
- Fear of adults of the same sex as the abuser
- Siblings behaving like boyfriend and girlfriend or embarrassed when seen together

Box 2.3
Some Indicators of Kids with Addicted Parents

Fear/mistrust of authority figures

Difficulty having fun

Judging oneself harshly all the time

Chronic anxiety

Secretive nature

Manifestation of physical symptoms*

Lack of self-respect

Compulsive lying

Feeling of alienation; "different" from others

Impulsivity

Inability to allow close friendships

*These kids often display physical symptoms related to extreme stress, such as explosive emotions, stomachaches, headaches, fatigue, etc.

Substance abuse by parents may also impact children and adolescents in more subtle ways. Timmen and Cermack (1985) described a condition which they referred to as "psychic numbing," or a sense of estrangement—a sense of being detached to the point of feeling there is no place or group to which one truly belongs. Such children are usually quite limited in their ability to express intimacy, tenderness, and even sexuality. Further, these feelings of isolation may lead to aberrant behavior many years later, or even suicide at some later point.

In many households that include drug-addicted parents, the children have to essentially raise themselves. In these cases, the children not only fend for themselves but may also take on a "caregiving" role relative to their own parents, which is a complete reversal of the traditional family roles. Further, perhaps the most damaging factor of parental drug addiction is the fact that many children living with substance-abusing parents begin to feel that their parents' addiction is somehow their own fault (American Addiction Centers, 2018). They may feel that, had they behaved better or done better in school, their parents may not have become addicted. While this is, of course, not true, the feelings often persist and can be quite damaging to the children emotionally. Box 2.3 presents some additional indicators that teachers might observe in students being raised by addicted parents.

Clinical Depression and Suicide

Major depression, sometimes referred to as clinical depression, is defined as a mental disorder characterized by at least two weeks of persistent low mood that seems to be independent of situations or setting. While major depression in childhood is rare, such depression is more common in children after puberty and in adolescents, and is frequently related to various anxieties. Clinical depression may also lead to suicide attempts. Because depression is more common as children mature into adolescents, the relationship between depression and suicide becomes more critical as children grow older. Still, not all children who contemplate or attempt suicide are depressed, and not all depression leads to suicide attempts.

Children whose parents manifest clinical depression are at a greater risk of being depressed themselves. Further, depression affects all ages, races, and social groups. Depression impacts both genders, but research has shown that girls are more likely to develop depression during adolescence than are boys (ADAA, 2018). Finally, between 2% and 3% of children ages 6 to 12, and 6% to 8% of teens may have serious depression.

Resent research has shown that the suicide rate among children and adolescents is increasing (Holmes, 2017; Vazquez, 2018). Fortunately, however, not all children or teens who think about suicide actually undertake a suicide attempt. "Suicidal ideation" involves the contemplation of suicide, and sometimes such ideation may involve an actual suicide plan, or broad idea on how to undertake suicide. In contrast, attempted suicide involves actual actions undertaken with the express purpose of doing oneself bodily harm or causing death. Finally, most attempted suicides are not successful, although the method used does influence the success rate of suicide. For example, guns are more lethal than drug overdoses when used for suicide.

Suicidal ideation, attempts, and completions also vary by age and sex. According to the Centers for Disease Control and Prevention (CDC), no suicide deaths were reported over a six-year period from 2008 through 2014 for children under the age of five. However, in the five- to nine-year-old group, and the 10- to 14-year-old group, suicide rates increased. Suicide rates typically peak between late adolescence and the mid 30s. Also, whereas girls are more likely to attempt suicide, boys follow through to completion more often. Suicide is the second leading cause of death for children, adolescents, and young adults from ages 5 to 24.

Teachers, social workers, and all mental health professionals have an obligation to be aware of the indicators that a child may be considering

Box 2.4

Signs of Potential Suicide and Suicidal Ideation

Family history of suicide attempts

Impulsivity

Feelings of helplessness

Bullying

Frequent or pervasive sadness

Decline in quality of schoolwork

Giving away personal items

Heavy social media use

Physical symptoms*

Exposure to or threats of violence

Aggressive or disruptive behavior

Loss or rejection

Changes in eating or sleeping habits

Withdrawal from friends, family, and regular activities

Unusual interest in dying

Increase in reckless behaviors

Changes (increase or decrease) in social media use

*Many kids with challenges in their lives display physical symptoms related to extreme stress, such as explosive emotions, stomachaches, headaches, fatigue, etc.

suicide, and these indicators are similar to the indicators for depression. Box 2.4 presents various signs that teachers can look for which may indicate that a child or adolescent is considering suicide.

Of course, if any of these signs are noted, the teacher should investigate the matter further by simply talking with the child or teen. Teachers might simply say, "How are you feeling today?" or "You don't look happy. Is everything okay?" Depending on the child's openness, this might be followed with more direct questions such as, "Have you ever thought about hurting yourself?" If any of these questions cause any concern, the teacher must report the concern to the appropriate school authority, usually a psychologist or counselor.

Naming the Beast

So ultimately, what is this beast—this constellation of potential childhood horrors that may or may not result in brokenness? Is there a single term or concept that captures the intricate relationships between all of these negative childhood experiences, a term which, hopefully, might provide additional insight into these kids? Can we name this beast, and will that help guide us in teaching them?

At least one large-data study can perhaps help us name the beast that causes such damaging brokenness among both school children and young adults. Felitti and his colleagues (1998), working with the CDC and Kaiser Permanente Health, surveyed a large sample of approximately 13,000 adults who had completed a medical evaluation and health survey at a large health maintenance organization. Just over 70% (9,508 people) responded by returning the survey. The survey sought information on seven categories of adverse childhood trauma, including psychological, physical, or sexual abuse; violence against mother; or living with household members who were substance abusers, mentally ill, or suicidal; or information on imprisonment of self and family members. The number of these negative childhood experiences was then compared with adult outcomes such as risky sexual behaviors, illegal drug involvement, health status, and disease.

Their first finding was staggering: over 50% of the adults in this study reported having experienced at least one type of adverse childhood experience, a percentage much higher than they expected. Further, 25% of these adults reported having experienced two or more of these traumatic events. Again, these data suggest that exposure to childhood trauma is much more prevalent than was previously thought. Also, further analysis of the data showed a distinct "graded effect" between exposure to childhood trauma and negative adult outcomes. Adults who had experienced four or more negative childhood traumas had 4- to 12-fold increased health risks for alcoholism, drug abuse, depression, and suicide attempts. They also had a 2- to 4-fold increase in smoking, poor self-rated health, more than 50 sexual intercourse partners, and sexually transmitted disease. A graded effect was likewise shown between exposure to childhood traumas and the presence of adult diseases including obesity, heart disease, cancer, chronic lung disease, skeletal fractures, and liver disease.

Over 50% of adults reported having experienced at least one type of adverse childhood experience, and 25% reported having two or more childhood traumas.

With these data from such a large-scale study showing clear indicators of brokenness among adults, the beast can finally be named: it is childhood trauma. We can now see that repeated trauma causes more brokenness. This study showed the many faces of horrid events to which children can be exposed and suggested that half of the adult population has some exposure to these traumas in childhood. Further, the graded outcomes by which increased exposure to childhood trauma related to increasingly negative adult outcomes shows a clear picture: repeated trauma can and often does result in brokenness, and increased trauma leads to still more negative outcomes. In this book,

Our beast now has a name: repeated, frequent childhood trauma causes brokenness.

I will continue to speak of both trauma and brokenness, but at the very least, our beast now has a name: repeated, frequent childhood trauma causes brokenness.

Broken Kids in My Class!

So what types of classroom behaviors do we see resulting from the repeated trauma described previously? The simple answer is anything and everything. For example, years of child sexual abuse may have created a person who engages in frequent, or even daily, sex, and often risky sex with virtual strangers. In contrast, the same type of abuse even over the same timeframe may cause another individual to shut down completely, to have virtually no sexual experiences, or even attempt to live in virtual isolation, never opening to anyone, under any condition.

Years of physical abuse may cause total incapacitation, an inability to hold a job or succeed in school, or may simply cause one to become a bully oneself, always seeking ways to victimize others. In short, the same risk factors, or the same traumas, may cause multiple behavioral manifestations—many layers of brokenness, if you will. Further, in most cases, the same "warning signs" may indicate various types of abuse or victimization, and those similarities can be seen in the various lists of indicators above.

In short, the same risk factors or the same traumas may cause multiple behavioral manifestations, or many different layers of brokenness.

In light of those difficulties in identifying broken kids, we must remember that the vast majority of kids who misbehave, even those who misbehave often, are not broken in the sense in which I'm using that word in this book. Brokenness is a condition resulting from life-threatening, highly emotionally damaging, multiple, and long-term trauma to which the young child or adolescent is exposed. These traumas may include severe and long-occurring abuse or sexual abuse, neglect, parental addiction, severe depression over a period of time, and so forth. These are the children who will require much more assistance, and typically this will include therapy by a highly trained psychologist or counselor, as well as a caring, understanding teacher.

Brokenness is a condition resulting from life-threatening, highly emotionally damaging, multiple, and long-term trauma to which a young child or adolescent is exposed.

With these characteristics noted, along with the observations from the previous chapter, we can list a number of characteristics of broken kids,

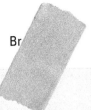

Box 2.5
Presenting Characteristics of Broken Kids

Broken kids demonstrate the following:

Never trust anyone

Often show fierce pride

Rarely or never apologize (it shows weakness)

Never celebrate their own achievements

Occasionally are explosively hostile

Seek perfect fairness and resent unfairness

Often show discomfort in social situations

Have few friends

Frequently refuse help even when needed

Never ask for help

Show little or no emotion

Frequently aggressive

Harsh judgments of self and others

Resist any physical closeness (hugs, etc.)

almost all of which were reflected by the broken adults described in chapter 1. Box 2.5 presents these presenting characteristics of broken kids. This is a quick, admittedly oversimplified picture of the results of severe, repeated childhood trauma.

However, in addition to these characteristics, there is one overriding characteristic to discuss—the issue of control. I had the opportunity when writing this book to describe this chapter with one of my personal confidants—a broken adult who actually lived through several of these devastating events during her childhood. She informed me that the single biggest issue for herself, and most of these other broken children or young adults, is control—an ability and/or the repeated attempts to personally control or even influence one's environment. This is an overwhelming motivation for broken people. She then shared several additional telling points.

First, she said to imagine a typical second-grade student's response to a teacher's discipline in the classroom. That typical student is quite used to disciplinary guidance from parents or other adults—those adults are physically larger and are believed by the child to be more knowledgeable and to have the child's best interest at heart. In short, those kids feel loved, cared for, and generally secure, and mostly they trust adults to not hurt them. As one example, in order to have dinner the previous evening, that typical second-grade child probably was called to the table and presented with a prepared meal. While at that meal, the typical child might be asked questions about his or her day at school, or about what reading they did, or what they talked about. There would be smiles and maybe even hugs for that child from a caring, involved parent. These experiences, on a daily basis, would result in the typical second-grader trusting the adults in the world, by and large, and thus accepting disciplinary interventions and perhaps even punishments in the usual way—maybe with some brief rebellion or "I didn't do it" type of response, but with a general acceptance of the punishment over time.

My confidant then contrasted that scenario with her own background. She said that when she and her siblings at that age wanted something to eat, they found whatever they could in the kitchen and ate. In her case, Mom was often gone, passed out from drug use, or entertaining some gentleman in the bedroom with the door shut. Any intrusion into that room resulted in curses or hitting, so the kids didn't disturb Mom in that situation. Also, my confidant stated that physical abuse was such a constant in her childhood that should someone touch her, she always cringed from fear. That response is still with her and often leads to problems in her adult relationships. In her world, and the world of most broken people, control of the environment was critical to self-preservation; control is everything! This woman and her siblings fixed their own meals since before she could remember. They bathed themselves from the early years, and they were ultimately taken into a series of group homes or foster homes, which might be either a blessing or another special type of hell. In short, in her world, if you could not control the world to some degree, even in the sense of hiding from a parent, or leaving the house when violence occurred, then abuse and physical pain would result. This young woman, and most broken people, will always be a "control freak," and the reasons are quite understandable. Control of one's world means survival!

My confidant then made one more interesting point. She said that if teachers could only understand the need for control among these broken students, they could then influence the students much more effectively. Specifically, she said that teachers must allow kids who have had to fend for themselves some control in the classroom, because control is such a dominant issue for these broken children. Choice in assignments is one excellent way to reach these kids. Further, teachers should make the point to these kids that education—doing well in their schoolwork—ultimately leads to much more control over one's own life. She stated that this could be, and in her experience was, quite a motivating factor, and it led her to strive to accomplish more in the elementary classroom and in her own subsequent schooling. While this young woman was trapped in a dead-end minimum wage job for a time after high school, I am very pleased to say that she is now completing her second year of a two-year college degree and is satisfied in the knowledge that her education will, in fact, lead to a job she wants and ultimately to more control of her own life.

So What Do I Do with These Kids?

Ultimately, teachers must take responsibility for these kids, and they may well ask, beyond vigilant observation of these various characteristics and behavioral indicators, "How do I help broken kids?" The mandate for teachers dealing with broken kids is rather simple to state but is very difficult to accomplish. Simply put, teachers must find, reach, and teach broken kids.

> *Teachers must find, reach, and teach broken kids.*

Of course, the simplicity of this statement drastically misrepresents the challenges for teachers dealing with broken kids. In finding these students, teachers must become aware of the types of sudden behavior change indicators that can suggest various underlying problems at home or emotional problems in the child. Establishing trust is even more challenging with these children, and once they have been found, and after some basis for mutual trust is established, the teacher must still teach them, leading them through the curriculum requirements as they would any other child. Again, none of this is easy!

Finding Broken Kids

With that noted, finding broken kids is less challenging than reaching them or teaching them. In many cases, broken kids are identified well before the school years, and if not, their behavior is quite noticeable once they reach school! Children who have endured these extreme levels of repeated childhood trauma are quite likely to have been previously identified, and they may already be seeing a counselor or psychologist. However, teachers should still be constantly aware, and vigilantly observant, since life circumstances for children can and do change (e.g., with parents' divorce and new people introduced into their lives). Also, broken children can and often do "slip through the cracks," particularly if their behavior problems are more subtle.

Further, many abused kids are "coached" by their abuser to not share their experiences with others outside the home. Thus, even teachers in later grades should carefully observe children in their care, watching for these indicators listed previously.

If a teacher suspects any of these childhood insults or problems, he or she is obligated to report them to the authorities in the school. Depending on the state or district, this usually means reporting the problem to a school administrator, psychologist, or counselor. When making such a report, I encourage teachers to write down the specific behaviors that made them suspect one of the problems, and hand that written statement to the appropriate authorities. The statement should include not specific allegations against parents or anyone else, but only the specifics on the behavior or statements by the child that made the teacher suspect a problem might exist. At that point, the appropriate authorities will take the lead in exploring the suspected problem and, if one is found, providing counseling or other services to the child.

Reaching Broken Kids

Once a problem is documented, the teacher has the responsibility to reach the child, regardless of what the problem or issue might be. Teachers, of course, are not trained therapists and should not attempt "therapy" with these broken children. With that stated, it is a fact that an elementary child will spend 20 to 30 hours weekly with their teacher but probably only spends 50 minutes weekly with a therapist or counselor, if they are receiving counseling at all. Thus, it is quite possible, if not likely, that the teacher becomes closer to the child than a psychologist or counselor. In those cases, the child may wish to open up more with the teacher, if they open up to any degree at all.

A child will spend 20 to 30 hours weekly with their teacher but probably only spends 50 minutes weekly with a therapist, so the teacher may become closer to the child than a psychologist or counselor.

Therefore, teachers should attempt to establish some level of trust with the children who may have these challenges in their background. Consistency during one's interactions with the child, a calm and measured response to every behavior the child exhibits, and a willingness to openly talk with the child can go a long way to help the child feel comfortable with the teacher, and should foster some degree of openness. Teachers should realize that even small steps toward a more open relationship represent huge successes with broken kids, since they will tend to be much more secretive than other kids. For some of these children, trust is the defining issue, but it will take time to establish a comfortable and trusting relationship.

Box 2.6
Guidelines for Reaching Broken Kids

- Learn more about all risk factors that cause brokenness and their impact on children.
- Reflect on every child presenting behavioral concerns in the class, asking the question, "Is this 'normal' misbehavior or does this represent a deeper problem?"
- Help broken kids to learn to take care of themselves. Talk about taking care of "yourself" in class. These kids must understand that it is okay to think about their own safety when faced with dangerous situations.
- Help broken kids learn to have fun.
- Help broken kids understand unconditional love. I believe that putting the concept of unconditional love in a religious context can be helpful, depending on the child's religious background and school policy.
- Talk with broken kids to earn their trust. Talk about good behavior, and about honesty and its rewards.
- Talk with broken kids about risky behaviors in an age-appropriate manner, and why they are dangerous.
- Help broken kids and adolescents find appropriate structured support groups where they can share their experiences with others.

Further, should such a trusting relationship become a reality, the teacher must be cognizant of certain limits of his or her training. Again, most teachers are not qualified as therapists for children with these types of severe challenges. Thus, the teacher must respect the limits of his or her training, and not exceed those limits. If information of therapeutic import arises in talking with a child, the teacher should report all such information to the counselor or psychologist at the school, who may then choose to share that information with the child's therapist. Box 2.6 provides additional suggestions for helping teachers reach out to broken children.

Teaching Broken Kids

Teaching broken kids involves moving the kids through the curriculum in such a way that continues to develop a trusting relationship and allows

Box 2.7
Broken Kids' Classroom Needs

Consistency in disciplinary policies

Written, posted rules to follow, developed with the input of the children in the class

Consistent consequences for misbehavior

Choices of assignments to allow these children some control in the classroom

Choices among punishments when needed

A highly structured daily plan and work schedule with only a few essential variations

Clear work expectations from the teacher

Explicit, directive communications from the teacher

Classwide and one-to-one discussions on disciplinary issues

A firm, fair approach to issues that arise in class

Time (and a strategy) to help students calm themselves after a problem arises

A genuineness from the teacher, which will help establish mutual trust

A willingness from the teacher to talk with these broken kids as problems arise

A private communication mechanism between teacher and student, such as hand signals or journal entries, to facilitate open but private communication

A degree of sensitivity when critiquing a child's schoolwork

A willingness to make exceptions for broken kids at times and to treat them differently from others in the class on occasion

for increased control by the child over his or her environment. With such control, a more trusting relationship can increasingly develop, thus allowing for increased growth of the child. Finding teaching activities and strategies that allow for children's choices, and increased openness and trust, should thus guide the teaching process. Box 2.7 lists some specific classroom needs that broken kids have, and most of these suggest specific ideas for teaching that can be accomplished with some extra time and work by a caring classroom teacher.

Summary

The reflections in chapter 1 and the factual data presented in this chapter paint a picture of who these broken kids are and identify some potential causes of brokenness. These children have been repeatedly exposed to trauma, in most cases over a fairly long period of time. As a result of these traumatic experiences, these broken kids will act and respond differently in the classroom.

In response, teachers must identify, reach, and teach these students. A number of indicators of problems have been presented that teachers should watch for, as well as some general guidelines for instructional planning and interactions with these children, which should help teachers in managing them in the classroom.

With that noted, broken children and adolescents—indeed, all victims of extensive and long-term trauma—will need much more attention and time than other students, even students who show consistent behavior problems. For most broken children, some type of therapy will be needed, and teachers must keep the therapist informed about changes in behavior, mood, or emotion shown by these children. At times, broken children and adolescents may be receiving medications for some of these problems, and teachers will need to closely monitor the impact of the treatments on the child's work in the classroom.

Next, in addition to the general guidelines presented herein, there are a number of specific teaching strategies that can greatly assist broken children. For purposes of clarity, I use the term "teaching guideline" when an idea can be summed up in a sentence or two, and a number of such guidelines have been presented in this chapter. In contrast, a teaching strategy is a more involved teaching approach that takes longer to describe as well as to implement. Each of the remaining chapters in this book will be dedicated to one teaching strategy that addresses the specific needs of broken kids.

To emphasize the importance of these teaching strategies, one caution for all educators is in order. With many children, perhaps as many as 15% or 20% of all children, being exposed to repeated childhood trauma, schools simply must do more to address the needs of these broken kids. Further, no educator should believe that the general guidelines in Box 2.7 are enough to address these children's needs. Rather, all schools should immediately consider the specific, highly involved instructional strategies presented in subsequent chapters of this book, and select the one or two that seem to be the best fit for your faculty. Absent the implementation of any of these strategies at the school level, the needs of these deeply broken kids will not be met, and that is an outcome no educator can live with.

CHAPTER 3

Traumatized Kids and Trauma- Informed Schools

The Basics of Trauma-Informed Schools

As noted throughout this book, broken kids have typically become broken by consistent, repeated exposure to trauma over a period of time (Craig, 2005; Felitti et al., 1998). Therefore, helping both teachers and the kids themselves understand trauma, and how trauma impacts various individuals, can be critical to any efforts to improve the children's mental health. The newly coined term "trauma informed" is used to describe teachers and school faculties who have received some training on trauma awareness, and schools in which students are taught to prepare for, survive, and emotionally deal with trauma (Adams, 2014; Craig, 2005; Lippman & Schmitz, 2013; Simmons-Duffin, 2018).

> *A trauma-informed school is a school in which teachers have received some training on trauma awareness and in which students are taught to prepare for, survive, and emotionally deal with trauma.*

To get an immediate picture of a trauma-informed school, I'd suggest that readers review one or several of the *YouTube* videos on this strategy; several of these can be found in Box 3.1. Also, the website from the Wisconsin Department of Public Instruction provides a list of resources on childhood trauma (http://www.traumainformedcareproject.org/resources/bibliography%20of%20resources%20for%20schools%20to%20be%20trauma%20informed.PDF).

Box 3.1
Video Examples of Trauma-Informed Schools

Office for Victims of Crime: Children, Violence, and Trauma—Interventions in School (https://www.youtube.com/watch?v=49GzqPP7YYk)

This video discusses trauma training in schools with educators at a number of schools in the US. This training is based on CBITS: Cognitive Behavior Intervention for Trauma in Schools, which is a 10-week intervention for individual and group sessions on making trauma bearable (e.g., relaxation strategies, ways to cope with anxiety, problem-solving skills).

Fall-Hamilton Elementary: Transitioning to Trauma-Informed Practices to Support Learning (https://www.youtube.com/watch?v=iydalwamBtg)

This video shows a single school in Nashville, TN, which follows both teachers and children as they become trauma informed. Strategies such as "peace corners," "check-in/check-out daily goals," and "classroom color and lighting" are explained as one way to increase the peacefulness in school.

EducationalImpact: Creating a Trauma-Informed School (https://www.youtube.com/watch?v=8MvueCKD2I0)

This video presents a trauma training program by EducationalImpact that shows how student misbehavior can be managed through trauma-informed disciplinary strategies.

Trauma-Sensitive Schools: Why We Need Trauma-Sensitive Schools (https://www.youtube.com/watch?v=vyQdOLI6d2c)

This video discusses how home-based trauma can be addressed in the school setting for immigrant children.

Trauma and Brain Functioning

The first step in becoming a trauma-informed school is developing understanding of brain functioning and how childhood trauma may impact brain functioning (Craig, 2017; Perry, 2014). The human brain is designed to change itself, with each change reflecting exposure to events in the environment, so it is clear that a child's brain will reflect the world in which they have been raised (Doidge, 2007). If their world is characterized by violence, verbal threats, unpredictability, fear, and trauma, the child's brain will reflect that by altering the development of the neural systems involved in the stress, aggression, and fear response (Chemtob, Novaco, Hamada, Gross, & Smith, 1997; Craig, 2017; Perry, 2000). In short, some children's brains have become "wired for trauma."

Of course, brain development and brain functioning go hand in hand, and both begin in the womb. Further, human brains are even more sensitive to, and reactive to, their environment at young ages. The fact that some very young children are frequently exposed to trauma will alter brain development, which in turn will impact both brain functioning and behavior at early ages and many years later (Doidge, 2007; Rosenthal, 2018). Further, Craig (2005, 2017) notes that childhood trauma may impact the young brain even before language is developed, and thus, these children during the later school years are less than capable when it comes to expressing themselves about certain fears, events, or situations that they perceive as related to the earlier traumatic insult. Likewise, the right hemisphere of the brain may be differentially impacted by childhood insult (Craig, 2017), and this may add to the inability of a child to answer certain questions like, "Why did you do that? What's wrong?" simply because language had not been developed when their brains were first repeatedly exposed to trauma. Hasn't virtually every veteran teacher been confronted with a situation in which a child was asked a question along these lines, only to be confronted with a child who is, seemingly, incapable of answering?

While extensive understanding of all brain functioning is not a reasonable expectation for teachers, having some insight into how a traumatized child's brain may respond can help a teacher to understand why children do what they do, particularly when their responses seem to be far outside the norm (Craig, 2017). To illustrate several possible impacts of trauma on children's brains, Box 3.2 presents some examples of traumatic brain insults and later behavior patterns that might be associated with them.

What Should We Teach Children about the Brain?

Of course, in addition to ensuring that teachers know a bit about brain functioning, trauma-informed teachers are teaching the fundamentals about brain functioning to children from the lower elementary years and up (Craig, 2017; Rosenthal, 2018). This instruction can empower children to learn different responses to perceived threats, and this will help decrease aggression and overt violence in many children over time. There are several concepts that can help in this regard, and each is described in the following sections.

Box 3.2

Brain Trauma and Related School Behaviors

Examples of Childhood Trauma	Aberrant Classroom Behaviors
Child suffers physical abuse to right hemisphere before age of 2 when language develops.	Child hits another kid in grade 4, and Teacher asks, "Why did you do that?"
Neural connections associated with violence made before the child can speak.	Child cannot answer. They have no verbal memory to answer (Craig, 2017).
Child exposed to sexual abuse from age 5 until 14. Neural connections develop that connect physical proximity with fear and pain.	Any time someone is behind or near the child, the child becomes agitated. If the child is touched, she might flinch or hit back.
Child is in a car accident that damages the hippocampus, which increases the stress hormone glucocorticoid. This might kill brain cells associated with memory connections.	Child hears screaming car tires, and jumps under desk to protect himself, not realizing that the threat is long past (Rosenthal, 2018).
Child fearful of abuse at home. Sympathetic nervous system highly activated resulting in a constant elevation of hormones associated with stress.	Child frequently tired and falls asleep in class nearly every day. Hard to wake up (Rosenthal, 2018).

The Three-Part Brain and Brain Functions

Using the concept of the three major brain functional areas, teachers should initially teach children a bit on how their brains function and how those brain functions impact their own thoughts and behavior (Craig, 2017; Rosenthal, 2018). A simple explanation of brain function is the triune brain, presented in Box 3.3. Although this model of brain functioning has been challenged as somewhat inaccurate or over simplistic recently, it has become the most frequently used model for explaining basic brain functions to children and teenagers.

Box 3.3
The Triune Brain

Reptilian Brain (lower brain functions): This innermost part of the brain and brain stem matures first. This is a brain component that humans have in common with reptiles, but reptiles do not have other higher function brain areas. This is the brain area responsible for survival instincts, aggression, and automatic body processes (e.g., heart beating and breathing without having to think about it). This brain area always searches for danger, as do reptiles, and these brain functions take over when any threat is perceived. This helps ensure survival of the organism. Most aggressive behavior stems from this brain component; kids who were traumatized early in life probably made unconscious life-long decisions about how to interact with the world, or how to react to threats, using mainly this brain region, because this region was more developed when the trauma occurred. Thus, these kids tend to be much more aggressive than normal, and they tend to believe that such aggression is normal.

Limbic System: The midbrain or limbic system is the midlevel of the brain, and it processes emotions. The limbic system is associated with social and nurturing behaviors and mutual reciprocity, and it conveys sensory data. Older students might also be taught about the *amygdala*, the part of the limbic system that controls emotions by tagging senses, memories, and emotions together. For example, the smell of hot apple pie may always elicit the emotional sense of entering Mom's kitchen during a holiday! However, after repeated trauma, the amygdala can get caught up in a highly emotional, alert arousal status; a type of "activated loop" of thought, during which this brain-activated loop looks for and perceives threats constantly and everywhere. Traumatized and neglected kids may be caught up in this "loop" of thought so that many things that are not threats are perceived as threats.

Forebrain and Neocortex (smart part brain): The most highly evolved part of the brain (our smart part). This brain region controls our thinking, cognitive processing, planning, decision making, reflection, reasoned judgment, language, learning, and memory. Although functional from an early age, this brain structure matures only in the early adult years (ages 22 through 24). Using these brain functions in times of stress frees us from exclusive use of the reptile brain and helps us make good decisions.

In teaching about these brain parts, teachers might point out that the "reptilian brain" controls our survival instincts—such as running away from something or defending ourselves by fighting. Thus, when kids want to hit someone, it is usually because their reptilian brain has taken control. In the context of the classroom, we should teach all children that instead of being controlled by the reptilian brain, we can use other sections of our brain—our smart part—to "talk to ourselves" and then choose a better course of action. Even young kids can understand that talking themselves out of being angry will help them get into trouble much less often. This *YouTube* video (https://www.youtube.com/watch?v=a_hPelcPRTg) provides an example of this instruction in an elementary class.

Neurons that Fire Together, Wire Together

This old adage states that sets of neurons firing together will increase the likelihood of the same neuronal set firing together again (or "wiring together"). Thus, the set becomes the "go-to" brain response to a specific situation (Craig, 2017). For example, suppose a complex set of neurons fired together each time a child was physically hit prior to the age of two and the development of expressive language. Those neurons might dictate a thought in the child's brain that goes something like this: "I've been hit—run or hit back!" Of course, that single thought would probably not be represented in language because most of those traumatic episodes took place before language was developed. Still, had that child been exposed to repeated physical violence at a very young age, then that particular neuronal set may well be so strongly connected (i.e., wired together), that the child displays the same aggressive and/or hitting behavior whenever he or she feels threatened in any way. A constant, frequent practice of rage yields constant expressions of rage in the human brain, and those expressions become hardwired over time.

The resulting aggression can easily show up many years later, when a child is 10 or 15 and in your classroom. In most cases, the child's aggression or violence will seem to be entirely out of proportion to the circumstances. Teachers must understand that broken kids do not need to actually *be hit* for that set of neuronal connections to fire. Rather, the child merely needs to perceive a possible threat of violence and he or she will then begin to hit back. Any perceived threat may elicit the violent hitting reaction from such a child.

Again when a child, particularly a child widely exposed to trauma, feels threatened, the reptilian brain takes control, shutting down other brain functions and shifting the brain and body into a reactive, fight-or-flee mode (Perry, 2014; Rosenthal, 2018). This scenario can and often does lead to out-of-control behaviors in the classroom. For this reason, teachers simply must strive to teach traumatized children to use their smart part brain, and thus activate other, higher brain functions, which can then be used when a threat is perceived.

> *When a traumatized child feels threatened, the reptilian brain takes control, shutting down other brain functions to some degree and shifting the brain and body into a reactive, fight-or-flee mode.*

Neuroplasticity

Neuroplasticity is the concept that brains can "heal" themselves; that they are "plastic" and can, with practice, develop the neuron connections to represent new and more advanced learning. It was once believed that neuronal connections, once established, were virtually fixed for life, but brain research over recent decades has helped scientists discard that notion (Doidge, 2007). Brain functions are amazingly malleable, and new learning, represented by new neuronal connections, can be developed at any point throughout life.

For children and adolescents exposed to drug addictions, childhood trauma, or other risk factors, this rewiring of the brain can be a long, arduous task, but brains can and do recover from many types of traumatic insult. New neural connections can be formed, and new behaviors in response to threats can be learned. This aspect of brain research should be emphasized, because the concept of neuroplasticity represents the hope that highly traumatized children can learn new brain connections that allow them to function in a more mature (i.e., "smart part") manner (Doidge, 2007). We must let traumatized students know that firing a "smart part" neuron set will strengthen that smart part brain connection over time, and this will help them stay in control of themselves much better and thus stay out of trouble.

Teach What Trauma Does to a Brain

In an age-appropriate way, trauma-informed teachers should teach broken kids about how trauma impacts their own brains. As one might imagine, this must be done with great sensitivity because this will involve ultimately teaching children that their brains are "wired" differently from the brains of other students. For children who have been repeatedly traumatized, teachers should, carefully and with great sensitivity, help them understand that their brains are "programmed" for aggression and violent behavior, programmed differently from other kids. Teachers must let them know that this probably explains why they sometimes feel different, or maybe even why they might seem to get into trouble at school more often than other kids. However, we should quickly emphasize that they can learn to develop increased control over their own moods and emotions, as discussed in the previous section on neuroplasticity.

Because this knowledge can potentially hurt or embarrass some children, this matter must be managed very carefully, and privately, by a trauma-informed teacher. I recommend that teachers hold this type of discussion with traumatized children with some caution, but it can be very important because many of these broken kids *know* that they are different. They may even be wondering "What's wrong with me?" In working with both broken kids and adults, I've heard this same question quite often, and providing an accurate, scientific answer sometimes helps put these folks more at ease. Again, the end of this discussion must heavily stress the "good news" that brains can and will learn to rewire themselves as they increasingly experience peaceful life situations and develop control over their moods and emotions. In fact, for some broken kids, this discussion can be the very moment that turns their life around.

If a child or young adult asks this question, after I've discussed basic brain functioning with them a bit, I typically say something like:

> *"Because of what you've gone through in life, you might see things differently from some other people, and this might cause your brain to react differently. Sometimes you might be more likely to fight or get angry than others, because that is what your brain is used to doing. That might be the reason you get into trouble a lot. Still, your brain is always changing and responding to the circumstances in your life, just like it should. The good news is that, as things get more and more peaceful for you here in school, you will learn to control your anger much more, and you will find that it is easier to maintain control without getting angry. I think your brain is doing that right now, so all in all, your brain is doing just great!"*

When the question, "Why am I angry all the time?" is handled in that fashion, most students will understand that they can learn to behave in a way in which they do not feel such persistent anger, and consequently they won't get into trouble as frequently.

What Else Do Trauma-Informed Schools Do?

At this point, we've discussed a number of things that schools should do to become trauma-informed schools. These include:

Ensuring that teachers know warning signs for various types of childhood trauma

Ensuring that teachers are informed about the impact of childhood trauma on behavior

Ensuring that teachers can, with sensitivity, teach kids about traumatized brains

Ensuring that teachers teach broken kids that they can control their moods and emotions

In addition to these practices, trauma-informed schools tend to emphasize teaching practices that are much more appropriate for traumatized brains (Craig, 2017). A few of these practices are described in the following sections, and others are included in subsequent chapters.

Establish a Calming Corner

Traumatized children tend to be highly reactive to stimuli, which may be perceived as threatening. Therefore, feeling safe is a huge issue because many kids do not experience that feeling in their own homes. For this reason, trauma-informed schools typically establish a "quiet corner," "peace corner," or "calming corner" in every classroom (Craig, 2017). This may be as simple as a rug, a comfortable rocking chair, or an inviting cushion on the floor in the corner of the room. The calming corner allows students to escape from the class for two or three minutes at any time they choose.

Students should be taught to retreat to the calming corner when they feel angry, frightened, or nervous. This will allow the child to begin to de-escalate and will thus help the child develop a sense of control over his or her fears or other threatening emotions. When a teacher sees a student in the calming corner, the teacher should make a point of allowing two or three minutes for the student to calm down and then walk over to ask, "Is everything OK now, or can I help?"

Offer the Students Choices

As noted previously, control is a huge issue for broken kids, and teachers can foster a sense of control over one's environment by offering choices whenever possible. Teachers have long realized that providing choices of assignments helps elicit more compliance and harder work in completing the assignments for all students; however, for traumatized children, who sense that they have little control overall, such choices can have a much more positive impact (Perry, 2014). Choices among assignments and other choices in school will tend to increase a child's sense of self-control (Perry, 2014) and typically will result in improved behavior in the classroom.

Perry (2014) also recommended structuring disciplinary consequences as choices for traumatized kids. When a child is noncompliant, the teacher should frame the consequence as a choice for the student. The teacher might say something like, "You have a choice. You can choose to do what I have asked, or you can choose to lose five minutes of your recess time (or other negative consequence)." Framing the interaction as a choice gives the student some sense of control and might help defuse the situation.

Emphasize Organizational Thinking

The traumatized child in a class, or, if you will, the traumatized brain, tends to be more disorganized than others. For many broken kids, the chaos and/ or violence of their childhood probably seemed totally out of their control and entirely haphazard. For most of these kids, there was no development of any sense of cause and effect, or any ability to predict violence in their chaotic home. For this reason, traumatized children do not grasp these organizational concepts as quickly or as easily as other children (Craig, 2017).

For broken kids, the chaos and/or violence of their childhood seemed totally out of their control and entirely haphazard. There was no sense of cause and effect, or any ability to predict violence in their chaotic home.

Craig (2017) emphasizes the use of teaching practices that stress organizational skills and the ability to internally organize knowledge. Of course, these same practices are, in most cases, best practices for all students. Teaching activities that stress organizational concepts such as estimation, prediction, patterns, or cause and effect, as well as reflective thinking at the end of a lesson, should be used whenever possible. Students need to develop the ability to understand and order knowledge internally, and this will take more work with traumatized kids than with others (Craig, 2017).

Use Questions that Stress Organization and Brain Functioning

Also, the teacher may emphasize such organizational thinking even when no specific prediction or estimation activity is planned merely by using appropriate question strategies (Craig, 2017). In a history lesson, for example, the teacher might ask about cause and effect or motivation by saying something like, "Why do you think Washington decided to cross the Delaware River and attack the British on Christmas Day? What did Washington hope to accomplish with that attack, and did he succeed?" These questions should elicit the cause-and-effect thinking that traumatized students need, since Washington's crossing did result both in a badly needed victory and in the re-enlistment of many soldiers in his army.

Further, Craig (2017) suggests that once we teach kids about brain functions, we emphasize brain functions throughout our lessons. In the example above, the teacher could continue the questioning about Washington by saying, "Okay, when Washington decided to go ahead with that attack, did he make that decision quickly and impulsively, or did he think about it? What part of his brain helped him make that decision?"

Teach Using Movement

In response to the emphasis on brain-compatible instruction over the last two decades, the importance of movement has been stressed for classrooms across the grade levels (Bender, 2012; Sousa, 2009). Movement has long been recommended as a teaching tool in elementary classes, and many examples are provided in the literature. Thus, most teachers today are using movement to represent concepts in the curriculum from kindergarten through elementary school. Further, numerous proponents have provided examples of movement-based instruction in middle and high school classes (Bender, 2012; Sousa, 2009). Thus, I will not provide additional examples here. Still, I should point out that highly traumatized brains tend to respond very positively to movement-based instruction (Craig, 2017) because movement can have a calming effect. Movement-based teaching will help children who are always stressed to relax more easily in the school environment.

Summary

Becoming a trauma-informed school is step one in meeting the needs of broken kids. As shown in each previous chapter of this book, highly traumatized children and adolescents will have varied and unique needs that simply cannot be met in traditional classrooms because traumatized brains are, literally, wired differently. In order to make any inroads with these broken kids, schools simply have to do more and must strive to become trauma informed. Although many techniques may be used that are effective with these highly traumatized students, this chapter has presented only a brief overview of the strategies that can be utilized. Later chapters in this book will focus on additional specific teaching strategies and ideas for teachers to implement in their efforts to adequately meet the needs of these broken kids.

CHAPTER 4
Social-Emotional Learning

The Basics of Social-Emotional Learning

Social-emotional learning (SEL) includes a number of emphases, and different proponents provide varying perspectives on what SEL actually is (Adams, 2014; Craig, 2017; Goleman, 1995; Lippman & Schmitz, 2013; Simmons-Duffin, 2018). Programs as varied as social skills programs (Cooke et al., 2007) to meditation programs (Black, Milam, & Sussman, 2009) are considered SEL, depending on which proponent is writing a given article (Durlak, Weissberg, Dymnicki, Taylor, & Schellinger, 2011; Vega, 2017). Still, undergirding the SEL construct are at least two emphases, emotional intelligence and resilience, and each of these will be discussed in turn.

Emotional Intelligence

Beginning with Daniel Goleman's 1995 book, *Emotional Intelligence*, schools in the US and around the world have placed more emphasis on developing the child socially and emotionally. In Goleman's view, highly developed skills, such as empathy, interpretation of social cues, and the ability to identify one's own emotions and ultimately exert control over them, may be defined as "emotional intelligence." His central thesis was that emotional intelligence probably impacts overall success in life more than either IQ or academic ability, since one's ability to self-regulate one's emotions and get along well with others often dictates one's success in the working environment as well as in all social relationships.

Emotional intelligence, therefore, is often defined as the capability of someone to recognize and exert control over their own moods and emotions,

Emotional intelligence is often defined as the capability of someone to recognize and exert control over their own moods and emotions, and to recognize the emotions and moods of others, and the capability to use this knowledge to guide their thinking and behavior to facilitate their efficacy in life.

and to recognize the emotions and moods of others, and the capability to use this knowledge to guide their thinking and behavior to facilitate their efficacy in life (Goleman, 1995). In this definition, one can see the numerous implications for broken kids, whose strongest motivation is to develop increased self-efficacy and control over their own life situation. As this concept of emotional intelligence took root in education, schools began to look for ways to help students enhance skills in this vast array of areas.

Of note in this definition is the rather elastic nature of the SEL concept. Because of this all-encompassing nature of the construct, the supporting research includes everything from evaluation of social skills programs to mood awareness activities in kindergarten. In spite of the broad nature of the construct, the instructional approach is useful for determining how to assist repeatedly traumatized kids, who may have significant deficits in any of these areas.

Resilience

More recently, in considering how to teach children and adolescents with behavioral problems, the concept of resilience has grown in influence (Lippman & Schmitz, 2013). Resilience, in the most basic sense, is one's ability to bounce back from negative life circumstances, and while the idea was developed among psychologists and educators to help children with abnormal behaviors or emotional problems, this idea is now guiding much of the thinking when it comes to highly traumatized kids as well. Many factors can help kids bounce back from less-than-adequate life circumstances, such as those discussed in chapter 2, and psychologists have used the term "resilience factors" to describe these things that potentially can foster resilience.

Resilience, in the most basic sense, is one's ability to bounce back from negative circumstances.

According to Lippman and Schmitz (2013), resistance factors include all of the attitudes, practices, and beliefs that foster resilience in children and adolescents. These include the following:

- Physical health supports resilience, including getting enough sleep, eating well, exercising, and enjoying good health;

- Social and emotional competencies that promote resilience, including stress management; a sense of control over one's life; a positive relationship to self, such as a sense of self-efficacy, self-regulation, and self-esteem; hopefulness and goal-setting with the motivation and perseverance needed to reach those goals; and social competence; and

- Cognitive competencies that help include insightfulness and general skills such as problem-solving, information processing, and intellectual ability.

Coupled with these individual attributes, attitudes, practices, and beliefs, these researchers likewise emphasize a variety of outside supports, either within the family or the community, which will help foster resilience in children (Lippman & Schmitz, 2013). These include things like a supportive family; effective parenting skills; the presence of a caring adult outside the family, such as a teacher, coach, or counselor; and membership in various social organizations such as school clubs, scouts, or age-appropriate religious groups (Adams, 2014; Lippman & Schmitz, 2013; Simmons-Duffin, 2018).

Given this array of resilience factors, one can note the appropriateness of using the concept of resilience in relation to highly traumatized kids. In fact, the resilience factors above read like a litany of life circumstances that were generally absent in the early lives of broken kids. Of course, some of these factors can be addressed by the schools, whereas others cannot. Although educators do play a role (as discussed in chapter 2) in watching for and identifying some forms of childhood trauma, such as child sex abuse or neglect, they are virtually powerless when it comes to protecting children from other risk factors (e.g., poverty or dysfunctional parenting in the home environment). Still, research on childhood resilience has shown that one caring adult in the community can be the resilience factor that allows a child to succeed even when exposed to several other risk factors (Felitti et al., 1998; Lippman & Schmitz, 2013). Clearly, schools can and often do provide such an adult role model for at-risk children, and subsequent strategies in this book (i.e., adult mentoring) will focus on another strategy for fostering childhood resilience in that fashion.

Finally, we should note that this resilience concept fits nicely with the idea of emotional intelligence. For both adults and school students, developing one's emotional intelligence facilitates one's ability to empathize with others and to use that empathy to better interpret and navigate emotional and social interactions with peers. The literature on this concept stresses that these skills will lead to increased success in life for all students. However, from the perspective of traumatized children, emotional intelligence can be seen as even more critical, because developing these skills will, in all likelihood, fill a deficit of such skills among these traumatized kids. Thus, emotional intelligence is a "resilience factor" and helps broken kids bounce back from repeated trauma or other less-than-positive environmental circumstances in the home.

Social-Emotional Learning

Based on both emotional intelligence and resilience constructs, SEL is a concept and a movement in psychology and education stressing emotional and mental health as critically important for students' long-term development and overall success in life (Belfield et al., 2015; Craig, 2017; Goleman, 1995; Lippman & Schmitz, 2013). Social-emotional learning is the effort to develop students' knowledge and skills in managing emotions, building healthy relationships, developing positive social skills and relationships, building resiliency, and making good life choices regarding participation in risky behaviors such as early sexual experiences, bullying, and drug abuse (Belfield et al., 2015).

> *Social-emotional learning is the effort to develop students' knowledge and skills in managing emotions, building healthy relationships, developing positive social skills and relationships, building resiliency, and making good life choices regarding participation in risky behaviors such as early sexual experiences, bullying, and drug abuse.*

In addition to this definition, most authors in this area stress five key competencies as the primary bases for SEL (Durlak et al., 2011; Shriver & Bridgeland, 2015; Taylor, Oberle, Durlak, & Weissberg, 2017; Vega, 2017). A quick review of those key competencies will, once again, show the broad nature of the SEL concept. Those key competencies, as summarized by Vega (2017), are presented in Box 4.1.

To get a more comprehensive understanding of SEL, educators should consider what this looks like in an actual classroom. Several video examples are presented in Box 4.2.

Given these broad competencies, educators will quickly realize that this concept of SEL encompasses many individual skills that were not included in the traditional school curriculum. Further, these competencies may be taught with a variety of techniques ranging from in-class discussions of moods and emotions to service learning programs within the community. Finally, because of the broad nature of this construct, several instructional approaches that may be considered SEL are presented independently in this book in subsequent chapters, including mindfulness, journaling, and service learning.

Box 4.1

Key Competencies for Social-Emotional Learning

1. Self-Awareness:
   - What are my thoughts and feelings?
   - What causes those thoughts and feelings?
   - How can I express my thoughts and feelings respectfully?
2. Self-Management:
   - What different responses can I have to an event?
   - How can I respond to an event as constructively as possible?
3. Social Awareness:
   - How can I better understand other people's thoughts and feelings?
   - How can I better understand why people feel and think the way they do?
4. Relationship Skills:
   - How can I adjust my actions so that my interactions with others turn out well?
   - How can I communicate my expectations to other people?
   - How can I communicate with other people to understand and manage their expectations of me?
5. Responsible Decision Making:
   - What consequences will my actions have on myself and others?
   - How do my choices align with my values?
   - How can I solve problems creatively?

Strategies to Teach Social-Emotional Intelligence

Teacher Tools

A wide variety of instructional strategies has been developed in recent decades to help students cultivate awareness of and control over their emotions and moods. For example, some kindergarten and early elementary teachers use a "mood wheel" to help students understand their different moods. A mood wheel (sometimes called an emotion wheel) can be used to help children begin to identify their own moods and emotions. A mood wheel may be easily constructed with laminated paper as the wheel itself, and on that paper the

Box 4.2

Video Examples of Social-Emotional Learning

Kids Matter Australia: The Five Social and Emotional Competencies (https://www.youtube.com/watch?v=pWZeR1bB038)

This video shows examples from the classroom that are associated with the five key competences.

Committee for Children: Social-Emotional Learning: What Is SEL and Why It Matters (https://www.youtube.com/watch?v=ikehX9o1Jbl)

This short video presents a definition of social-emotional learning, and uses avatars made of clay to illustrate each point, so this can be shared with young students but is appropriate with students of all ages.

Edutopia: 5 Keys to Social and Emotional Learning Success (https://www.youtube.com/watch?v=DqNn9qWo01M)

Using real kids, this video presents a number of educators discussing social-emotional learning.

teacher writes down words representing different moods or emotions (*angry, depressed, fearful, uncomfortable, happy, excited, very interested*, etc.).

For young children in the pre-reading years, an emoji may be pictured on the wheel beside the term itself. Another sheet of laminated paper with a picture of a selection arrow could then be affixed to the wheel, allowing children to spin the wheel to select the emotion or mood they are feeling at that moment. A picture of a mood wheel is presented in Figure 4.1. Also, teachers can find more information on mood wheels and even download a printable wheel from the following site: https://childhood101.com/helping -children-manage-big-emotions-my-emotions-wheel-printable/

Teachers may have a wheel at each child's desk or one large wheel in the front of the room (or both). Once each child has a mood wheel, the teacher can instruct all students to identify their mood first thing in the morning and leave the wheel visible on the top of their desk. Then, should that mood change, the teacher might teach the children to reset the mood wheel to reflect the changed mood. At any point, should a child indicate he or she is angry or very depressed, the teacher should make time to have a quick discussion with

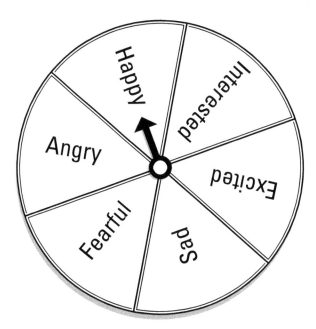

Figure 4.1. Mood Wheel

that child to see what the problem might be. The purpose here is not to do in-depth therapy with every mood change but merely to get children used to identifying and labeling their own moods and emotions. This is, of course, the first step to controlling them.

The anger thermometer is another way to help students gauge their moods. Sousa (2009) described an example of an anger thermometer on which moods were described on a prioritized scale ranging from "Feeling peaceful and ready to work" to "Feeling angry and too upset to do anything." Another example is shown in Figure 4.2, and kids can show their level of anger by moving a paper clip from one level to the next. When explaining the anger thermometer to students, the teacher might state that students can choose, to some degree, what they feel, and that "feeling frustrated" might be better than feeling angry. In fact, "feeling frustrated" rather than "feeling anger" might result in a child having more control over a given situation. Having children describe their moods as progressive states can help even very young children understand that moods and emotions sometimes build upon each other, but that the child can exercise some control by cautioning oneself to not jump immediately into anger and rage. Activities such as these allow students to assess their own moods and emotions and ultimately gain control over them, resulting in improved self-regulation of moods and decreased anger and aggression (Davis, 2015).

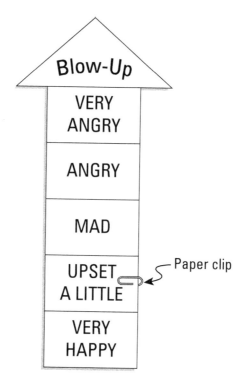

Figure 4.2. Anger Thermometer

Published Programs and Curricula

Beyond the individual teacher developed ideas above, a number of published curricula have been developed for teaching SEL, and many have received research support (Belfield et al., 2015; Cooke et al., 2007; Upshur, Heyman, & Wenz-Gross, 2017). Of course, given the array of emphases within the SEL concept, not all curricula include all of the five key competencies. Still, a description of one such curricula will help teachers understand the types of SEL available.

One curricula that has been the focus of SEL research is *Second Step* (https://www.secondstep.org/). As described by Cooke et al. (2007), the *Second Step* curriculum emphasizes the following skills:

Impulse control—the ability to control and manage thoughts, feelings, and behaviors, including listening, focusing attention, following directions, using self-talk, showing assertiveness, and identifying and understanding feelings.

Empathy—use of appropriate conversation skills, joining groups, making friends.

Emotional management—ability to calm oneself; manage anger; deal effectively with accusations, disappointment, and anxious or hurt feelings; resist revenge; and avoid jumping to conclusions.

Problem-solving—develop the ability to play fairly, take responsibility, solve classroom problems, solve peer exclusion problems, handle name calling, deal with peer pressure or gossip, and seek help when needed.

As these areas indicate, this program is fairly comprehensive and addresses many of the key competencies that define SEL. Implementation of *Second Step* usually involves a schoolwide effort and includes both teacher and parent training elements. Programs are available for early learning, elementary, and middle school; the *Second Step* program has been implemented in more than 26,000 schools worldwide. The class activities are available with each component of *Second Step* and are easily used in any classroom. Also, research cited on the company website as well as in numerous academic journals is strongly supportive of this program (Espelage, Low, Polanin, & Brown, 2013; Low, Cook, Smolkowski, & Buntain-Ricklefs, 2015; Upshur et al., 2017).

While the *Second Step* curriculum represents one example of SEL, many other curricula address aspects of SEL. Box 4.3 presents a brief annotated list of several of the more widely used curricula.

Research on Social-Emotional Learning

Almost all of the considerable body of research on SEL investigated the implementation of commercially available SEL curricula such as those in Box 4.3, rather than individual teacher-developed SEL activities such as the use of mood wheels. Still, the research on social-emotional interventions overall is quite positive and clearly shows that SEL works (Belfield, 2015; Cooke et al., 2007; Dodge et al., 2014; Durlak et al., 2011; Espelage et al., 2013; Jones, Brown, & Aber, 2011; Low et al., 2015; Shriver & Bridgeland, 2015; Taylor et al., 2017; Upshur et al., 2017; Vega, 2017).

The research on social-emotional interventions overall is quite positive and clearly shows that social-emotional learning works.

For example, research that investigated the impact of SEL on academic performance showed a positive impact (Belfield, 2015; Durlak et al., 2011; Jones et al., 2011; Oberle et al, 2017; Vega, 2017). In fact, one meta-analysis of 213 SEL programs found that social and emotional learning interventions increased students' academic performance by 11 percentile points (Durlak et al., 2011).

Box 4.3

Examples of Other Social-Emotional Learning Curricula

Responsive Classroom—This program is intended for use with students from kindergarten through grade 5 (https://www.responsiveclassroom.org/). The program uses morning meetings, positively stated school rules, positive redirection with logical consequences for inappropriate behavior, modeling role-playing and positive teacher language to teach appropriate behaviors. Research results have been positive for this program (Vega, 2017).

4Rs—This program is one of the more widely used social-emotional learning curricula (Vega, 2017) and is intended for grades pre-K through 5. The 4Rs curriculum (Reading, Writing, Respect, and Resolution, https://www.morning sidecenter.org/about) helps children to develop empathy, critical thinking skills, and conflict resolution skills. Jones et al. (2011) and other researchers have demonstrated the efficacy of this program in improving behavior, decreasing depression, and increasing academic scores.

Positive Action—This program is used from kindergarten through grade 12 (Vega, 2017; https://www.positiveaction.net/). Thinking through and completing positive actions in all situations is emphasized, and this program has demonstrated results in increased academic scores and improved behavior.

Unconditional Education—This is a school partnership model that focuses on partnering with schools in urban areas (http://www.unconditionaleducation.org/). This builds the school's capacity to meet the diverse academic, behavioral, and social-emotional needs of students across the age range (Vega, 2017).

Resilience Builder Program—This program is based on the book *Resilience Builder Program for Children and Adolescents* (2011) by Mary Karapetian Alvord, Bonnie Zucker, and Judy Johnson Grados. The book provides 30 group session lessons designed to help youth bounce back from challenges in their lives. The program is shown to increase confidence, self-esteem, and self-control, as well as the use of coping strategies. The lessons also stress development of self-regulation of emotions and behavior.

In addition to promoting academic improvement, the research generally supports use of SEL curricula to improve behavior and decrease depression, anxiety, and aggression of students in schools (Belfield et al., 2015; Durlak et al., 2011; Taylor et al., 2017). Although these results are generally robust, not all studies showed benefits in all areas of behavioral improvement. For example, Cooke et al. (2007) investigated the impact of the *Second Step* program with 741 students in grades 3 through 5 from six schools. After receiving the *Second Step* intervention, students showed significant improvements in areas such as caring-cooperative behavior, suppression of aggression, and consideration of others. However, this study revealed no changes in aggressive behavior or disciplinary referrals.

The research generally supports use of social-emotional learning curricula to improve behavior and decrease depression, anxiety, and aggression of students in schools.

Given the emphasis in this book on broken kids—highly traumatized students exhibiting extreme behavioral disruptions—these data suggest that more research is needed on the impact of SEL programs on this group of students. For example, perhaps there are positive benefits in behavioral areas among some students with certain types of behavioral problems but not among highly traumatized, broken kids, who may represent the extreme end of the behavioral disruption continuum.

With that caution noted, there are indicators in this body of research that SEL does have significant benefits even for repeatedly traumatized children. For example, the research shows that such training can help students develop empathy for others, improve attitudes toward others, improve regulation of moods, and decrease drug usage and other risky behaviors many years after the program is implemented (Dodge et al., 2014; Durlak, 2011; Jones et al., 2011; Taylor et al., 2017). Of course, these are some of the target behaviors that require immediate attention among broken kids. Thus, teachers dealing with this population are well advised to consider implementation of some type of social-emotional curriculum for these reasons.

It is interesting to note that the research on SEL is, in some ways more comprehensive than research on some other educational intervention areas. For example, a number of studies have investigated the long-term impact of social-emotional training (Dodge et al., 2014; Jones et al., 2011; Taylor et al., 2017). This body of research suggests that positive impacts of social-emotional training can be seen years after these school-based interventions are concluded. The results show benefit in terms of less illegal drug use, fewer social-emotional problems, and improved interpersonal skills (Dodge et al., 2014; Taylor et al., 2017). As one example, Dodge et al. (2014) studied 25-year-old former students who had received some form of SEL during their school years. The results showed that those young adults were 10% less likely than others to demonstrate psychological, behavioral, or substance abuse problems. Similarly, Taylor and his co-workers (2017) showed many of the same benefits of social-emotional interventions from six months up to 18 years after the intervention ended. This type of long-term follow-up is quite rare in most educational intervention areas.

Further, in one of the most interesting analysis of the long-term impact of SEL, Belfield and his coworkers (2015) investigated the economic impact of these interventions in a cost/benefit analysis—a type of research that is extremely uncommon in the educational literature. Results showed that, on average for every dollar spent on social-emotional interventions, there is a return of $11 over the early years of the young adults' lives. This, along with the results reported previously, documents that teachers should be implementing some type of SEL program in virtually all schools.

Action Research: A Case Study on Social-Emotional Learning

Providing research documenting the efficacy of a new instructional strategy is typically the responsibility of research scientists at universities, but teachers often do collect data on classroom-based instructional projects to show the efficacy of an instructional technique they have decided to begin using. Here is an example of this type of research, sometimes referred to as "action research."

Ms. Kay was very concerned about a child, Austin, in her fourth-grade class. He seemed to get frustrated and then angry virtually every day, and once he felt anger he seemed to lose control of his emotions. His behavior became extreme and sometimes violent at that point. She was unaware of any specific concerns in his home environment, but clearly he was not as mature as her other students in labeling and understanding his own emotions. Further, he seemed unable to regulate his emotional outbursts. He often ended up crying, and sometimes he began to hit students near him. Finally, he could get angry at almost anything, from not knowing the answer to a question, to a student across the room making a loud noise. Ms. Kay was not in a school that had implemented a schoolwide SEL program, so any intervention she chose to implement meant working on Austin's problems alone.

Still, Ms. Kay wanted an intervention that would help Austin identify, understand, and ultimately control his emotions, so she decided to use a simple social-emotional intervention discussed previously, the mood wheel.

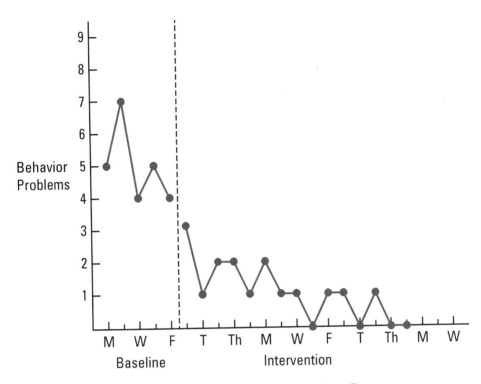

Figure 4.3. Austin's Mood Wheel Intervention Data

To begin, she kept a count of each instance in which Austin lost control of his moods and had to be called out for disciplinary reasons in class each day. She collected this baseline data for a week, as shown in Figure 4.3.

Next, to begin the mood wheel intervention, she made a large "mood wheel" for the entire class, and discussed the moods presented on the wheel with the class. She chose the following mood indicators:

Feeling just OK

Excited and ready to learn.

Very upset

Angry

Happy

Mildly upset about something.

Frustrated

Calming down

On the first intervention day, the class talked about the feelings that indicated particular moods and some of the things that might move kids toward one mood or another. Then, she made five "student sized" mood wheels and explained that each week, five different students would use the mood wheels. Each time their mood changed during the day, they would indicate that new mood on the mood wheel and, if Ms. Kay decided it was appropriate, the class would then briefly discuss that child's mood change.

With multiple students using the individual mood wheels, Austin was not particularly singled out in front of the class, but Ms. Kay made certain that Austin was in the first group of five students to use the mood wheel. Each morning, all five of the students were asked to "set" their mood wheel at "Excited and ready to learn" unless they felt something else. They were then told to reset their mood wheels when they felt a mood change and hold them up for Ms. Kay to see. She could then determine if the class should discuss the mood change, depending on classwork and other factors.

For Austin, Ms. Kay did not count the number of times his mood changed during a given day. Rather she counted the number of times he showed angry behavior overall, regardless of whether or not he used the mood wheel to label his mood change. With all five of the students, she made a point of discussing some of the mood changes, depending on the importance of the mood change and the time and ongoing activities in her class.

After the first week, Ms. Kay explained to the class that two of the five students using the mood wheel had done so well with it that they would continue to use the wheel, while the other three students would pass their mood wheel along to someone else. In that way, Austin continued to use his mood wheel for a second week.

These data show that during the first week, Austin began to reduce the number of times he showed anger, and by the second week, his anger outbursts were significantly reduced. He'd gone from an average of five outbursts daily to less than two, and Ms. Kay was particularly pleased to reach the end of the day on Thursday during the second intervention week and realize that she'd had no behavioral problem from Austin all that day!

Of course, this intervention did not eliminate Austin's behavioral problems, nor did it address his long-term emotional needs. However, it did make him much more "teachable" in the class, and often that type of small victory can be the basis of establishing a lasting trust with some broken kids. With these kids, all victories count!

Summary

Social-emotional learning has gone far beyond merely an instructional approach to assist with troubled kids and has now become a "cause" for many educators. When we consider the number of highly traumatized kids in schools today, one can easily understand why. As this brief summary shows, the research is strongly supportive of SEL, and while the overall area is quite broad, schools are lining up, and linking up, to create SEL school networks. At the very least, these innovative programs do provide a way for schools to address behavioral problems for many students, and this area shows the most potential to address the critical needs of even highly traumatized kids in schools today. For this reason, we might well expect some type of SEL implementation in virtually all schools at some point in the near future. Clearly, absent such an effort, schools will not be meeting the needs of many children, and particularly those of our broken kids, in our classrooms.

CHAPTER 5

Mindfulness for Broken Kids

Because broken kids manifest mood disorders, a lack of emotional self-regulation, and many different types of other emotional problems, helping these students understand that they can gain some control over their own moods and emotions can be one of the most important things we teach them. In fact, emotional self-regulation skills may be much more important for their long-term success than almost anything else in the school curriculum. One only need consider the question, "What good would total mastery of the school curriculum do for a broken kid if they are still an emotional train wreck?"

The growing mindfulness movement among schools worldwide provides an excellent teaching strategy which addresses many of these mood difficulties, emotional problems, and even the classroom behavioral problems of broken kids. With roots in both yoga and certain Buddhist meditation practices, mindfulness has become a widely accepted academic strategy in schools throughout the US and worldwide (Campbell, 2013; Cox 2015; Davis, 2015; Harris, 2015; Oaklander, 2015; Thomas, 2016). Further, many trauma-informed schools specifically implement some type of mindfulness program as one aspect of their help for broken children, while realizing that mindfulness well serves all children and adolescents in today's stressful world.

The mindfulness strategy involves providing students with a meditative time period, during which the student reflects on his or her emotional state and level of relaxation, in an effort to help the child better understand his or her moods and emotions. In turn, this new understanding can result in reduced stress, depression, and anxiety, as well as increased student attention (Campbell, 2013; Davis, 2015; Klatta, Harpsterb, Brownea, White, &

Mindfulness involves providing students with a meditative time period, during which the student reflects on his or her emotional state and level of relaxation, in an effort to help the child better understand his or her moods and emotions.

Case-Smith, 2013). Mindfulness also stresses recognition of and control over, one's emotional states and moods. Through these emphases, mindfulness practices are aimed directly at reducing stress and fostering peace of mind in order to empower students to be more in control of themselves and thus more readily available for learning (Albrecht, Albrecht, & Cohen, 2012).

Using mindfulness exercises, educators can teach students to assess their own emotional state, calm themselves down, concentrate on one thing at a time, and reflect more deeply on their work (Albrecht et al., 2012; Harris, 2015). Students can learn mindfulness techniques in as little as 15 minutes daily over a period of six to eight weeks, and such practices ultimately will have many benefits that directly address the many aberrant behaviors and emotional problems demonstrated by broken kids.

To actually see mindfulness exercises in real classrooms, I'd suggest that readers view one or more of the many videos on mindfulness in schools, which are listed in Box 5.1. Also, several mindfulness curricula are available for teachers, as described in Box 5.1. However, teachers should bear in mind that they can undertake implementation of mindfulness without using these curricula by reviewing free materials from *YouTube*, this book, and other such resources.

While mindfulness practices may seem somewhat esoteric, or perhaps even a bit too "new-age" for some veteran teachers, the practice has been expanding in schools around the world simply because it works! Furthermore, it seems to help all children and adolescents in school and not merely kids with severe emotional or behavioral problems, as attested to by many students themselves on various videos noted in Box 5.1.

Mindfulness practices evolved from yoga in the early 1970s as a way to boost energy and productivity (Davis, 2015). Mindfulness has since been employed by many organizations including Google, the United States Army, and the Seattle Seahawks football team (Davis, 2015), and today, many educators implement daily mindfulness exercises in their classrooms (Greenberg & Harris, 2012; Oaklander, 2015). Given this rather wide acceptance of mindfulness to reduce stress and help regulate mood, mindfulness is certainly something that can be recommended for all broken kids and indeed, as the research suggests, for all kids.

Box 5.1
Resources on Mindfulness in Schools

Videos of Mindfulness Practices in Classrooms

Mindful Schools: "What Is Mindfulness?"—Awakening Kindness and Curiosity at School (https://www.youtube.com/watch?v=uezOV_D8bSk)
In this video, both teachers and kids explain their mindfulness practice.

Peace in School: Powerful Video about Mindfulness in Schools (https://www.youtube.com/watch?v=cOGM_-zKPTE)
In this video, students in high school talk about the importance of mindfulness.

The Hawn Foundation: The MindUp Program (www.youtube.com/watch?v=tAo_ZSmjLJ4)
Actress Goldie Hawn promotes mindfulness in schools.

Mindfulness in Schools: Mindfulness and the Brain for Children (https://www.youtube.com/watch?v=a_hPeIcPRTg)
In this video, mindfulness and the brain are explained to elementary children.

CBS This Morning: Baltimore students get meditation, not detention (https://www.youtube.com/watch?v=SpjWb9teKSY)
In this video, young children are taught to do a mindful moment, which decreased class disruptions for an entire school.

Mindfulness Curricula Used in Schools

MindUP (https://mindup.org): The MindUP curriculum is promoted by Goldie Hawn and the Hawn Foundation. It is one of the most frequently used mindfulness curricula in schools and is founded on four pillars: neuroscience, mindful awareness, positive psychology, and social-emotional learning. Students learn to quiet their minds in three-minute brain breaks three times daily: first thing in the morning, after lunch, and before leaving school. Teachers can download a guide at the website.

Mindful Schools (www.mindfulschools.org): The Mindful Schools program is another program frequently used by teachers. This program can be purchased online, along with mindfulness training for teachers. The six-week online course costs $125 and provides the basics of mindfulness meditation, techniques for navigating intense emotions, and a series of role-plays on mindfulness and communication.

Mindfulness in an Inner-City High School Class

Here's an example of mindfulness implemented in a high school in the Bronx, one of the poorest inner-city districts in New York City (Davis, 2015). In this school, located in a district where the average family is challenged economically, mindfulness was embraced by students and teachers alike. Argos Gonzalez taught an English class with a mix of black and Hispanic students. When the class began, Gonzalez rang a bell and said, "Today we're going to talk about mindfulness. You guys remember what mindfulness is?" When no one spoke, Gonzalez gestured to one of the posters pasted at the back of the classroom that summarized an earlier lesson on mindfulness. In the earlier lesson, the students had brainstormed the meaning of mindfulness and listed some phrases such as "being focused," "being aware of surroundings," and "being aware of my feelings and emotions."

Gonzalez continued with the following instructions: "I'm going to say a couple of words to you. You're not literally going to feel that emotion, but the word is going to trigger something; it's going to make you think of something or feel something. Try to explore it. First, sit up straight, put your feet flat on the ground. Let your eyes close."

Gonzalez then tapped the bell again, and the class became quiet. Then he said, "Take a deep breath into your belly. As you breathe in and breathe out, notice that your breath is going to be stronger in a certain part of your body. Maybe it's your belly, your chest, or your nose. We'll begin with trying to silently count to 10 breaths. If you get lost in thought, it's okay. Just come back and count again. Whether you get up to 10 or not doesn't really matter. It's just a way to focus your mind." Then the students practiced that mindfulness activity for several minutes (Davis, 2015).

Teachers around the world, like Gonzalez, are choosing to spend 10 to 15 minutes of precious class time daily on this type of procedure for one simple reason: Mindfulness strengthens the kids' learning and self-control to a point where less time is taken on mindfulness exercises than would be expended on managing a child's behavior problems were the mindfulness program not in place. Teachers would not invest this time unless the benefits were clearly evident in their own class (Davis, 2015).

Mindfulness strengthens the kids' self-control to a point where less time is taken on mindfulness exercises than would be expended on managing a child's behavior problems.

In fact, teachers using mindfulness constantly report increased productivity and fewer behavior problems among the students and a better class climate when they practice mindfulness with the students (Albrecht et al., 2012; Greenberg & Harris, 2012; Harris, 2015). Today, schools all across the United States and the United Kingdom are beginning to practice mindfulness daily in the classroom (Davis, 2015) because these benefits among all kids are so apparent, and those benefits would be particularly important for broken kids.

Implementing Mindfulness

In addition to the published curricula, there are many individually developed approaches to teaching mindfulness in medical, therapeutic, and classroom settings, and various approaches stress different things. These range from intentional breathing to self-awareness to walking meditations (Cox, 2015; Welham, 2014), and training is typically available from the organizations that develop mindfulness curricula.

The compilation of suggested procedures that follows come from a variety of sources (Caprino, 2014; Davis, 2015; Welham, 2014). While these are presented in no particular order, these activities do represent the types of mindfulness exercises that are being done in the classroom, and teachers should feel free to implement mindfulness training based on the information in this book and the examples one might find on *YouTube*. The description in the previous classroom example will also be of help. Here are some activities to do daily for five to 10 minutes.

Breathing Exercises

Breathing exercises were discussed in the previous classroom example, when Mr. Gonzalez had students count their breaths in a calm, soothing setting. Like Mr. Gonzalez, many teachers teach breathing exercises to focus students' attention and help them relax (Davis, 2015). Such relaxation will help reduce stress and even foster higher student engagement in subsequent academic periods.

Self-Regulation through Mood and Emotional Awareness Activities

As discussed in previous chapters, teachers in trauma informed schools teach students a bit about the human brain and regions of the brain associated with different types of moods and emotions (e.g., the amygdala as the emotional brain and the neocortex as the planning brain or smart part; see chapter 3). An example of such "brain training" for elementary students was shown in one of the videos recommended in Box 5.1. Students learn a bit about how their brains function and then refer to those brain regions while they explore their own moods and behaviors, or the moods and behavior of others (Welham, 2014). Over time, even students who have undergone significant long-term trauma can learn to exert influence on their own moods and emotions, and such self-regulation will help them achieve more balance in their lives overall. For example, some teachers use a "mood diary" (a technique that is self-explanatory) to help students focus on their feelings and moods daily.

Several examples from the previous chapter, such as the mood wheel and the anger thermometer, are activities that can help students develop awareness and control over their moods.

Senses and Sensory Experience Awareness Activities

Some mindfulness trainers have the students practice attention skills by stressing sensory stimuli. Students might be asked to chew a raisin (only one raisin) for an entire minute—chewing slowly and focusing their attention only on the sensation of chewing or how the raisin tastes. Alternatively, students might touch different textured cloths while they concentrate on the sensations with their eyes closed. Focused sensory awareness helps students with attention deficit problems.

Focused Awareness Activities

Focused awareness involves having students focus on doing only one thing at a time (e.g., walking, looking at nature, or completing a morning reading with no distractions or outside thoughts allowed). This will help students develop task persistence and focused attention.

Quiet-Time Stress-Reduction Activities

"Quiet time," or "three-minute meditation time," are terms used by schools to emphasize merely quietly breathing to reduce stress, and these exercises work over time for most children and adolescents (Oaklander, 2015; Schwartz, 2016). Several of the recommended videos show the use of quiet time, and this can be implemented by a single teacher in his or her classroom or by an entire school. Some teachers use a small bell as a signal for "meditation" or quiet time to begin and end, as shown in the example described previously. Once students have been shown what to do during quiet time, they generally go immediately into meditation for a two- or three-minute period at the sound of the bell, and then they come back more focused and ready to work. Many schools have experienced significant decreases in disciplinary problems through using quiet-time activities such as these (Davis, 2015).

Many parents might object to mindfulness instruction if mindfulness is approached as either yoga or religious instruction. However, by approaching mindfulness with a focus on quieting the minds to reduce stress, depression, and anxiety, as well as improving student well-being, teachers can usually forestall that potential parental concern. Of course, parents should be fully informed of this instructional focus and be assured that no religious training is taking place (Welham, 2014).

The Turtle Technique Relaxation Strategy

As early as the 1970s, various researchers saw a need for teaching very young students who were prone to aggression and violence in schools a relatively simple way to un-stress or de-escalate potentially violent situations. At that point, Schneider and his associates (Robin, Schneider, & Dolnick, 1976; Schneider, 1974) developed the Turtle Technique, a self-regulation technique that consists of three components: the turtle relaxation phase, a problem-solving phase, and peer support.

The image of a turtle withdrawing into its shell is explained as a protective space from which the turtle can stop interacting with the external environment. Young children are taught to withdraw into their shells by placing their heads on their desks, locking their arms under their heads, and closing their eyes (Robin et al., 1976). They are told that this is how the turtle protects itself and draws strength to face the outside world. While in the turtle position, children are taught to relax their muscles and ignore any sounds in the class while they begin to cope with any emotional tensions.

After a period of relaxation in the turtle position, the students might be asked to discuss with the teacher what happened and/or begin a series of problem-solving activities that allow the student to reflect on his or her behavior (Robin et al., 1976). The dialogue presented in Box 5.2 illustrates how young children may be taught this technique. Once they know the technique, young students are expected to "do a turtle" when they are feeling fear, rage, or anger. Also, teachers can request that students "do a turtle" when they perceive that a child is moving into a negative or violent mood.

Beyond teaching the turtle response itself, two additional aspects of this technique should be emphasized. First, after the relaxation, the student is to engage in some reflective problem solving concerning his or her behavior (Fleming, Ritchie, & Fleming, 1983; Robin et al., 1976). For example, in the study by Fleming and colleagues, four basic problem-solving steps were taught to the students: (1) identify the problem, (2) generate alternative solutions, (3) evaluate alternatives and select the most appropriate, and (4) implement

Box 5.2
Dialogue to Teach the Turtle Technique

"Little Turtle was a handsome young turtle very upset about going to school. He always got in trouble at school because he got into fights. Other kids would tease, bump, or hit him. He would get very angry and start big fights. The teacher would have to punish him. Then one day he met the big old tortoise, who told him that his shell was the secret answer to all his problems. The tortoise told Little Turtle to withdraw into his shell when he felt angry and rest until he was no longer angry. So he tried it the next day, and it worked. The teacher now smiled at him and he no longer got into big fights" (Robin, Schneider, & Dolnick, 1976).

the selected alternative. Then after doing a turtle, students would be expected to answer the questions in a discussion with the teacher.

Second, it is critical that the other members of the class respect the student's choice to become a "turtle" for a few moments. Thus, the Turtle Technique should be taught to all class members with the emphasis that, "When someone is in the turtle position, everybody else leaves them alone!" The class should be instructed not to talk to, joke with, or talk about the student who has chosen to withdraw into his or her shell.

The same idea, without the turtle example, can be used with kids up through grade 12. While use of the turtle metaphor itself should probably be limited to grades K through 4, older students may be taught the same technique by calling it a "time out." For example, students in secondary school may be encouraged to signal the teacher that they need a time out using the same time-out signal used in football. The student could then place their heads on their desks for a one-minute time out and momentarily escape from the social demands of the classroom. Both teachers and students should agree not to call on or ask questions of the student while he or she is in this time out.

Research on Mindfulness Training in Schools

Mindfulness has received general research support in a variety of areas in both the classroom and clinical settings (Albrecht et al., 2012; Campbell, 2013; Greenberg & Harris, 2011; Klatta et al., 2013; Schonert-Reichl, &

Lawlor, 2010; Schwartz, 2016; Semple, Reid, & Miller, 2005; Thomas, 2016). These studies indicate a number of positive benefits of mindfulness programs in schools, including reduced stress, improved regulation of one's own moods, improved capacity for compassion and empathy, decreased anxiety, decreased depression, decreased aggression in the classroom, and increased attention. Further, several studies have even reported increased academic scores resulting from mindfulness training (Albrecht et al., 2012; Oaklander, 2015). Finally, medical studies using brain-imaging techniques have shown that longer-term mindfulness training can result in thickening of the cortical regions of the brain related to attention and sensory processing. Clearly, this body of research demonstrates the potential of using mindfulness for students with attention-deficit/hyperactivity disorder, aggression, mood disorders, and other mental health problems; in short, virtually all broken kids.

One example of classroom-based action research on mindfulness was presented by Schwartz (2016). After implementation of daily mindfulness activities for a period of weeks at a K–8 school in Portland, Oregon, both teachers and students demonstrated clear benefits from mindfulness training. Data showed that office disciplinary referrals were decreased and that both teachers and students reported a drastically improved school climate as a result of the mindfulness program. In short, this and other research supports mindfulness as an effective strategy to reduce depression, stress, aggression, and anxiety while improving mood and emotional self-regulation, attention skills, and social skills.

Action Research: A Case Study on Mindfulness

Mr. Trenton had two children in his fourth-grade class who had suffered abuse as young children, and both were constantly disturbing the class with aggressive disciplinary outbursts, either verbal or physical. He had to stop class almost daily to deal with aggression from one, if not both, of these students. Mr. Trenton determined to try a mindfulness approach by using a daily "quiet reflection time." First, he gathered baseline data showing the number of aggressive or other behavioral problems of the two students (Mike and Darius) over a one-week period as shown in Figure 5.1.

These data show that during the first week, both Mike and Darius disrupted the class several times each day, so some intervention was necessary for each student. To do this intervention, Mr. Trenton began a "training week" during which he taught various mindfulness exercises, with each 10-minute training session followed by a three-minute meditation period. During the training sessions, Mr. Trenton talked with the children about different feelings, such as anger, frustration, depression, fear, happiness, joy, and so forth, and he

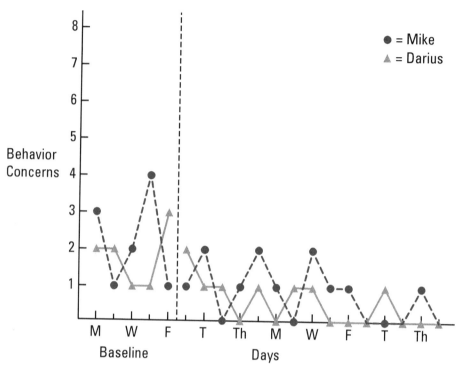

Figure 5.1. Disruptive Behaviors of Mike and Darius

illustrated each mood or emotion with a "face" picture showing the emotion or mood discussed. He urged the class to ask themselves, "How am I feeling?" and then indicate the face that most closely represented their feeling. This was intended to help students become aware of their feelings. Then, each day, he urged students to do a "mindful moment" (see an example of mindful moments at https://www.youtube.com/watch?v=SpjWb9teKSY), which is a quiet-time meditation that is similar to the breathing exercise used in the previous classroom example with Mr. Gonzalez. As in that class, Mr. Trenton tapped the edge of a metal bowl to make a ring sound to signal the beginning and end of the three-minute meditation.

During the training week, and for two weeks thereafter, Mr. Trenton continued to keep a chart of misbehaviors of both Darius and Mike. As the data show, the misbehaviors of these two students began to decline as soon as the training began and was reduced significantly by the end of the action research project. Total misbehaviors had been reduced from an average of 4.0 daily (between the two students) to 0.4 daily by the last week of the intervention. These data show how mindfulness exercises can work to reduce misbehavior over time. At the urging of his principal, Mr. Trenton then shared these data during the next faculty meeting.

Summary

The extant research suggests that mindfulness should be considered for implementation in practically all grade levels for most kids in schools, including broken kids. Further, teachers might explore using mindfulness in the specific subjects that tend to produce increased stress among students, such as science or mathematics. Both at the elementary level and in departmentalized schools in the upper grade levels, teachers are making time for mindfulness exercises and have repeatedly asserted that this is time well spent. For highly traumatized kids who are overcoming home-based challenges, a practice like mindfulness can be much more than merely a technique to improve behavior; it can literally be life-saving, as several students presented on the recommended videos have testified. In short, this will be time well spent and it may help save a child from severe depression, consistent anger, or suicide.

CHAPTER 6
Journaling

The Basics of Journaling

What Is Journaling?

Journaling, which is sometimes referred to as *expressive writing*, includes a variety of forms of written thought ranging from keeping a personal diary about feelings or situations in one's private life to writing down one's daily reflections on specific academic topics studied in school. Journaling, in the school context, usually involves a regularly scheduled time during which students write down their thoughts, feelings, and impressions, or summarize their daily lives, and those journal entries are typically reviewed by the teacher (Adams, 2018). *YouTube* presents a number of videos on journaling in grades kindergarten (a group activity) and up (see https://www.youtube .com/watch?v=sqySzZp2Hrs or https://www .youtube.com/watch?v=BHNICh8yGVY). Viewing one or more of these videos is recommended in order for the novice teacher to get a sense of what other teachers are doing in their journaling assignments.

> *Journaling involves a regularly scheduled time during which students write down their thoughts, feelings, and impressions, or summarize their daily lives, and those journal entries are then reviewed by the teacher.*

For academic journaling (e.g., a mathematics or social studies journal), the teacher might make required assignments within a particular subject or course, and students would be expected to write about the topic or discussion. However, most journaling in the school context involves topic-free journaling, in which students are provided the time to write in their "daily journal" and may talk about any topic they wish. For teachers dealing with broken kids, these open-ended journaling options are probably be the best choice because

> *For broken kids, open-ended journals are be the best choice because these journal assignments offer students the opportunity to communicate about their thoughts and feelings without limitation.*

these journal assignments offer students the opportunity to communicate about their thoughts and feelings without limitation and without the need to relate those feelings to a given topic or subject. Because of this advantage of open-ended or open-topic journals for broken kids, the remainder of our discussion herein will focus on those open-ended journaling assignments.

Depending on the specific situation, student journals may be either considered totally private or may be shared only with the teacher. While private journals do provide an opportunity for self-reflection for students, I generally recommend shared journals in which the teacher occasionally reviews journal entries. In most instances, teachers cannot review all journal entries for all students because time concerns are pressing for most teachers. However, reviewing some journal entries for all students is certainly time well spent. Also, encouraging the children to let the teacher know when he or she should review a particular journal entry is wise. When used in that manner, journals can become a relatively private and protected mechanism for communication between the teacher and the student.

For reaching broken kids (who, as noted previously, are at times seemingly unreachable), a journal can be the perfect self-reflection tool, and follow-up discussions with the teacher can become an important outlet for student emotion. Further, this use of student journaling does foster and encourage some trust between the teacher and the student.

The Benefits of Journaling

Many authors have noted the positive benefits of journaling for students of all ages (Finley, 2010; Greenawald, 2018; Lewis, 2017; Murray, 2002; Ullrich & Lutgendorf, 2002).

While this book is not primarily intended as a review of research on these teaching strategies, teachers should know that research on journaling, although not extensive, does document many positive benefits of journaling for broken kids. These include reducing stress, improving self-perceptions, improving writing and communication skills, and even strengthening the immune system (Dunlap, 2006; Fritson, 2008; Lewis, 2017; O'Connel & Dyment, 2006; Scott, 2018; Ullrich & Lutgendorf, 2002). Further, school journaling has been shown to be associated with decreases in clinical depression, anxiety, increases in positive moods, increases in social engagement, and improved quality of close relationships (Grothaus, 2015; Murray, 2002). Thus, this strategy has very real physical and mental health benefits for broken kids as well as all other kids in the class. Of course, the specific benefits of journaling are dependent on the seriousness of the student during the writing process. Still, journaling is a recommended procedure for students who suffer from stress, depression, and anxiety disorders and can be one tool to improve students' mental health and behavior overall (Fritson, 2008; Murray, 2002).

> *For broken kids, journaling holds many benefits including reducing stress, improving self-perceptions, improving writing and communication skills, and even strengthening the immune system.*

For many kids, including many troubled kids, it is not uncommon that deeply reflective and emotional thoughts emerge in the journal pages, and thus journals allow these students one opportunity to share their feelings, their deepest thoughts about the challenges within their lives. This is why journaling is often included in therapeutic treatment plans for both children and adults. Further, various sources have identified an array of other benefits of journaling for mental health, as presented in Box 6.1 (Lewis, 2017; Scott, 2018; Ullrich & Lutgendorf, 2002; University of Rochester Medical Center, 2018).

From the perspective of the teacher dealing with deeply broken kids, the positive impact of journaling on stress is critically important. In fact, not only does journaling reduce stress overall, it also improves immune system functioning at the biochemical level in the body (Fritson, 2008; Grothaus, 2015; Scott, 2018). This measurable physical result of journaling indicates the potential strength of this strategy for broken kids who have survived harsh challenges during their childhood. If physiological changes can and do result from journaling, it is easy to see that positive psychological changes such as stress reduction and increased relaxation can likewise result, as this research has consistently shown.

Further, because both trust and control are huge issues among broken children and adolescents, finding methods to encourage these students to share their thoughts, feelings, and fears is critical. With journaling, students do sense that they have some degree of control. In journaling assignments, the student is in control and any topic can be acceptable for the journal. Further, the student controls what is written down and what is not. Thus, the student can choose to trust the teacher as much or as little as he or she wishes. Once trust is established between the student and the teacher, the journal can

Box 6.1
Benefits of Journaling on Mental and Physical Health

Journaling can help one:

Manage anxiety

Cope with depression

Control stress related symptoms

Improve one's mood

Decrease symptoms of asthma and arthritis

Recognize/control triggers for depression or anxiety

Provide an opportunity for positive self-talk

Develop a plan to resolve one's problems to reduce stress

Improve the immune system functioning

Improve mobility among arthritis patients

Reduce one's stress

Understand one's moods

Improve cognitive functioning

Prioritize problems and fears

Track symptoms day to day

Identify negative thoughts/behaviors

Decrease blood pressure

Improve sleeping patterns

Help wounds heal faster

serve as a critically important communication mechanism for these students. Many students who might be embarrassed to share their experiences when talking with other students or their teachers may find that they can share those feelings by writing them down in a journal entry, even when they know the teacher will be reading the journal at a later time.

Finally, many kids who have faced challenges in their childhood display somewhat limited academic skills, and such limited ability is not uncommon amount students with challenges in their past. For students with limited writing ability, the talk-to-text feature available on modern computer programs will allow students to journal and thereby share their deepest feelings via talking about them at the computer. This feature is likewise available on most smart phones. This can extend the benefits of journaling into much lower grade levels, as well as to kids with academic delay in writing. Thus, journaling is strongly recommended for virtually all broken kids, including those in any grade between kindergarten and grade 12.

How Do I Do Journaling?

What Are the Types of Journaling?

Open-topic journals include a wide array of writing options. While merely making paper, pen, and writing time available to kids in the classroom can work for some students, more specific types of writing expectations that are topic free can help more reluctant students to begin the journal writing process. As one might guess, for many students who have experienced some failure in school as have many broken students, a blank page can be quite intimidating. Thus, having some structure to the journaling, without specifying specific topics for each journal entry, can be helpful for many students. Various authors have provided suggestions for the types of journals that may help students get started (Adams, 2018; Scott, 2018), and these types of journals entry ideas are presented in Box 6.2. While any of these can work, teachers should use a variety of these ideas for the journal assignments, and perhaps vary the journaling assignments from day to day, based on these various types of journaling entries.

Group Journal Writing

Most teachers implement journal writing as an individual task because the intent in journaling is to provide students with opportunities to share their deeper thoughts, emotions, and concerns. However, sometimes shared or partner writing journal activities can be of benefit (Adams, 2018). Working in groups of two or three, students might be required to jointly write in each other's journals, or to write in a shared journal, on a topic specified by one student or another. As one might imagine, this can help shy or reluctant students participate more in the journal writing process, since the social expectation in a shared journal writing assignment can motivate some students.

> *Working in groups of two or three, students might be required to jointly write in each other's journals, or to write in a shared journal, on a topic specified by one student or another.*

These types of shared writing experiences often promote higher participation and sharing of ideas. Creative teachers might even find ways to use social-networking platforms such as Twitter for this type of assignment, making group journaling particularly appealing to today's digital learners. Adams (2018) provided a series of ideas for journal writing that can be the basis for shared journal writing activities, as presented in Box 6.3.

Box 6.2

Types of Open-Journal Assignments

Gratitude Journal Entry. A journal entry that identifies three or more feelings or events each day for which students are grateful. For broken kids, this helps them focus on positive things in life and can provide a list of daily events which may be referred to in the future. They can then use this list to remind them of positive things when they are feeling down.

Emotional Release. In this type of journal, students write about things that were stressful, emotional, or even particularly enjoyable during their day. While these entries can focus on both positive and negative emotional events, the ratio of positive to negative is important to consider for stress reduction. The more positive things included in the journal, compared to negative things, the more positive students may feel overall. Teachers should discuss that ratio with the students, pointing out the benefits of positive journaling in terms of stress reduction (Scott, 2018).

Bullet Journal. A personal planning journal that lists in bullet form, the types of activities that a student must accomplish. For many individuals, being more organized in this fashion helps alleviate stress.

Sentence Stem. A stem sentence has long been used by teachers as a way to help reluctant writers write, and one or more such stems can help students in journaling. Stems such as "Right now I feel . . ." or "Today I was most happy when . . ." can help students get their feelings out (Adams, 2018).

Areas of Life Inventory. An inventory of various areas of life can focus students on what's going on in various areas. These may include stems such as "At school today, the most important thing was . . ." or "At home yesterday . . ." or "My feelings today were generally very. . . ." One could also include other areas such as work, spiritual, health, or family.

Clustering My Feelings/Thoughts. This type of journal entry or technique involves both writing and artistic creation. It involves writing down words or thoughts briefly, and then drawing connecting lines to show connections. This can focus on a core thought, issue, event from the day, or problem and then make connections with specific times or events during the day.

(Continued)

Box 6.2 *Continued*

Listing. Journaling can begin with listing ideas such as "Five things I enjoyed today . . ." or "Today my five biggest worries were . . ."

Captured Moments. This type of journal entry will focus on writing a brief vignette on a daily event. Ideas might include: "My best time today . . ." or "My happiest moment was when. . . ."

Unsent Letters. Students can be told to imagine a positive or negative thing they might wish to say to someone. Whereas sharing positive ideas or thoughts is always advisable, sometimes sharing negative thoughts can help students clarify thoughts. This is the advantage of having students write a letter that they will not send. Point out to the students that this writing process can help them understand their thoughts but that it is wise to not actually send such letters.

Box 6.3
Group Journal Writing Ideas

Alphabet Lines. Teachers begin this by writing the alphabet from A to Z vertically down the side of a page. Students should then be encouraged to write a poem or story in which each successive line begins with the next letter.

Dialogue. Two or three students might be encouraged to write an imaginary dialogue on a particular problem or situation. One student can suggest a topic or problem he or she is having, and others may be encouraged to write from differing perspective about the topic.

Character Sketch. Developing a character sketch in journaling is similar to describing a character in a story. Working together, students might be required to add to the character description based on their own experiences.

General Guidelines for Journaling

In addition to the types of journal ideas above, additional guidelines and tips for journaling have been provided in the literature to help teachers get started in the journaling process (Adams, 2018; Grothaus, 2015; Lewis, 2017; Scott, 2018; University of Rochester Medical Center, 2018). Initially, teachers should determine what types of time might be devoted to journaling, when it should take place, and how students should do their journaling. Additional guidelines that are particularly relevant for teachers who intend to use open-journal assignments with broken kids are presented in Box 6.4.

Cautions in Journaling

Research does raise several cautions in using journaling. Most of these questions deal with the time it takes to write or review journals, maximizing the positive impact of journaling, and managing dangerous or destructive issues that arise in journaling (Finley, 2010; Lewis, 2017; Stosny, 2013). In short, journaling can either help or hurt, depending on how this teaching approach is used (Stosny, 2013). Here are some suggestions to assist in these areas of caution.

Time Management for Journaling

Finding time to have students write in journals can be a challenge. Of course, the benefits of journaling are most readily realized when teachers make the time to allow students to write in their journals, and many elementary teachers find some time for daily writing (Lewis, 2017). For teachers who are concerned with time and are new to journaling, journal assignments can be given once or twice a week initially. Also, if pen and paper are the journal medium of choice, students can be encouraged to do additional journaling at home or whenever they feel like it.

While some time for daily journaling in the elementary class seems to many teachers to be possible, this issue is more pressing in departmentalized schools since it is hard to find journaling time within, say, a daily 55-minute algebra period. With that noted, topical academic journals may still be used in those departmentalized classes, and students can be encouraged to do journaling once or twice a week at the end of class, or even as a homework activity.

A more serious issue is how the teacher finds time to review journal entries. The benefits of journaling will not be realized unless the teacher makes time to reflectively review at least some of the journal entries on a regular basis, but I can almost hear my "veteran-teacher" readers asking, "Who has that kind of excess time in the classroom to devote to writing journal entries?"

Box 6.4
Guidelines for Keeping an Open-Topic Personal Journal

- Have students write every day if possible. Journaling can become quite engaging, so teachers should limit the time students have for journaling. Most teachers generally recommend from 10 to 20 minutes daily.
- Have students keep it simple. Students might keep a pen and paper handy at all times so that when they want to jot down thoughts, they can. Some students carry a small writing pad along with them all the time, and such journaling should be encouraged, even after school.
- Pick a writing medium that works in your class. Some argue that pen and paper are the best media for journaling, since these can go anywhere and there is evidence that the writing process with pen and paper stimulates certain brain regions more than work on a computer (Grothaus, 2015). Others suggest that journaling on a computer is best. I suggest you pick a medium that works in your class and stick with it. You might want to keep a journal in a computer file, as well as on a small pocket pad on your person.
- Have students write whatever feels right. Ultimately, this is their journal, and students should not have to worry about any particular structure, unless a structure is recommended to focus the class on one issue or to help students who are reluctant writers.
- Give some guidance on what to share. Some students are nervous about what they should share, but if the intention is to invite open communication between a teacher and a student with issues at home, let kids know that they should share anything about their feelings, lives, emotions, or home situations that they want the teacher to know. Also, invite students to let the teacher know when they write a particular journal entry that the student wants to discuss.
- Don't edit and don't grade! Journaling should be an occasion for the free flow of ideas, and words should flow freely from one's heart without worrying about spelling mistakes or what other people might think. Only students and teachers will see the journals, and while the teacher's natural inclination is to "correct" the journal, this is strongly discouraged because, at least for broken kids, teachers typically use journals as an open communication tool.

(Continued)

Box 6.4 *Continued*

- Share journal entries as the student wishes. Students might choose to share their journal with close friends, but they should be cautioned to remember that journals contain some of their deepest thoughts, and it is up to them whether or not they share with other students.
- Journal in the same place daily. For in-class journaling, have students pick a spot in the class (e.g., their desk, a comfortable rug, floor space) and journal in the same location daily. Getting students out of their desks, if other comfortable seating options are available, can facilitate the journaling process.
- Require a table of contents. Tables of contents can help students in long-term reflection on a given problem, particularly if they can find previous journal entries from weeks or months ago on the same issue. The table of contents will help in that process. Generally, students should add a few items to the table of contents every four or five days.
- Write teacher comments. While not all journal entries will be reviewed by the teacher all the time, when teachers do review journal entries they should make brief comments to encourage the students or ask questions about the entry. Likewise, some teachers encourage students to highlight or specifically identify any journal entries they want the teacher to read.

However, in considering the reality of teaching broken kids, I'd like to turn that question around: "Who can afford not to do journaling?" (Finley, 2010; Lewis, 2017). We know that journaling has many benefits for these kids, and thus journaling is quite likely to alleviate some of the extreme behavior problems demonstrated by broken kids in the classroom. It is possible that this activity actually saves teacher time, since prohibiting those misbehaviors via journaling may take less time than managing them once they occur. If some mechanism for sharing their deep thoughts and feelings is not provided to these students, veteran teachers can easily imagine the time they will have to spend in extreme disciplinary efforts for these broken kids! In short, isn't a journaling assignment, which can be done by all kids in the class, more beneficial than time spent responding to disciplinary problems for one or a few kids? In that regard, teachers will quickly see the benefits of journaling assignments for broken kids as well as others in the class.

Maximizing the Positive Impact of Journaling

For some students who undergo severe challenges in their home life, journals can become focused almost exclusively on negative events or challenging life circumstances, and thus journaling might seem to reinforce how horrible life can be (Stosny, 2013). To prevent this outcome, teachers should always encourage children to focus on some positive events, feelings, or experiences each day in the journal entry, along with teasing out the negative events or problematic situations. Further, even for negative events or emotions, having the student use those journal entries to both describe their thoughts and emotions and then to seek and identify some possible resolutions to the problem can transform even those negative journal entries into important learning opportunities.

Next, research has shown that journals can do harm to students if the activity makes students merely a passive observer or self-obsessed with horrible situations in life. Further, journals should not become vehicles of blame or merely list all the negative things in one's life (Stosny, 2013). Stosny urges teachers to make journaling a positive experience by helping students reflect on and evaluate their emotions as they explore solutions to various problems and issues. Students may be encouraged to convert negative energy into positive energy and to bring their negative emotions into alignment with their deepest core values.

When used in this fashion, journaling can help students lower their emotional reactivity to negative situations, and perhaps consider positive courses of action for some tough situations. Stosny (2013) provided a series of questions that teachers might use to help students develop positive journal entries and/or to positively reflect on negative events or feelings that come to light in journaling; these are presented in Box 6.5.

Not all of these questions should be addressed in every journal entry, but rather, these should be considered as students deal with tough or highly emotional events or situations. Having the student address some of these questions can turn a negative journal entry into a more positive experience for the child.

Handling Dangerous Events Described in Journal Entries

The final issue in using journals involves dealing with concerning or dangerous content that may come to light in journal entries. It should be obvious that traumatized children come from homes where something has gone terribly wrong, and one might expect for journal entries from troubled kids to reflect that reality. Sometimes, those journal entries might bring up legal matters such as abuse, violence in the home, other dangerous home conditions, dangerous thoughts such as harming oneself, or even suicidal ideation. In all

Box 6.5

Questions to Foster Positive Benefits in Journaling

Write a few sentences about a problem, event, situation, or negative feelings that you had.

- Try to look objectively at the thoughts, emotions, and behavior you expressed.
- Would you think the same if you felt comfortable?
- Can you convert the negative energy of this into positive creativity and growth?
- Are you acting according to your deepest values and the kind of person you want to be?
- How are your actions in this experience in keeping with your deepest values?
- Would you feel the same if you were firmly in touch with your core values?

Write a few sentences considering each of the following:

- What can you learn from this matter? Can you grow from this experience?
- How can what you learn make the world a better place and you a better person?
- Can you tolerate a certain amount of ambiguity or lack of clarity about this matter?
- Is it okay to have mixed feelings about the matter you described?
- Can you raise your confidence to deal with the worst case scenario should it occur?
- Do you have a plan of action should the worst case scenario happen?
- What are the perspectives of other people in your problem description?
- How would they describe the events?
- What core hurts might they be experiencing or avoiding (unimportant, guilty, devalued, powerless, inadequate, or unlovable)?
- Are you being as humane and compassionate as you want to be?
- Do you think the other people involved in this situation are more frail than cruel or evil?

Describe what you will do to improve the situation you described.

- Can you improve this situation?
- If you can't improve the situation, describe what you can do to improve your experience of it (i.e., how you can make it more pleasant or less uncomfortable for yourself).

probability, journal entries from broken kids are likely to raise such matters more frequently than journal entries from other students. Thus, teachers should consider what happens when dangerous emotions or reflections or even illegal events are described in children's journal entries.

Imagine a scenario in which a teacher reads the following journal entry of a fourth-grade boy:

"Last night Mom and her boyfriend were fighting, so I went to my room to play on the X box. When I heard a loud bang, I looked out my bedroom door and Mom was on the floor. Her nose was bleeding. I didn't see the guy, so I went back into my room, but I cried later that night."

With increased societal awareness of child abuse and neglect, teachers know that any suspicion of, or any hard evidence of, child abuse or neglect must be reported to school authorities, and school administration officials may then report those suspicions to police or other appropriate agencies. As discussed in chapter 2, most school districts have specific reporting forms for teachers or school administration officials to complete, and immediate reporting of these issues is demanded by law. However, in the scenario above, it is possible that the child experienced some trauma, while neither being abused nor neglected, since his journal entry does not show that he was directly involved in the altercation. In contrast, one might argue that being exposed to such violence is, in and of itself, traumatic child abuse. Still, the question remains: If a teacher sees this type of entry in a journal, what does the teacher do?

Because of the inherent challenges many children face, the factors that cause brokenness, children should be protected whenever any question arises. The safety and growth of the child must be the teacher's overriding concern, so for teachers who read a journal entry such as the one above, I'd suggest a discussion with the child about the situation described. One might ask the child, "What do you mean when you say 'fighting'? Were they arguing, or shouting, or did you see them hit each other?" Another question might be, "Do you think this man hit your mother and caused her nose to bleed, or did she fall against something that caused the nosebleed?" These questions can help understand what actually happened in the view of the child.

Further, questions that tease out the child's feelings are also useful. "Were you afraid when you cried that night? Did you think the man was coming back, or did you cry because your mother was unhappy?" Sometimes, questions about feelings can help the teacher understand if the child's fears are rational and are related to the specific, actual events. In fact, the child in the situation above may have cried because he or she watched a scary movie in the bedroom, and thus the crying may not be related to the adult argument at all. The journal entry merely stated that the child cried later, not that the crying was related to Mom's altercation.

I also suggest that the teacher write down the time, date, and the child's answer to whatever questions are asked. Those answers might become the basis for further inquiry by the appropriate authorities, if the child does, in fact, seem to be in danger.

In the case of a journal entry where there is some ambiguity, as in the case above, these questions should help provide the teacher with some direction, and again, the safety and growth of the child must be the overriding concern. When a child is not safe, and that is revealed in a journal entry, then the teacher must raise questions, using the journal entry and any notes on questions that were asked, as well as the child's answers, as the evidence for later inquiry. For first-year teachers, if the teacher feels some questions are warranted but is uneasy asking anything of the child based on his or her relative inexperience, he or she might merely take the journal entry to the school counselor or administrator and have that person ask questions of the child, and then determine a course of action. Again, the child's safety must be the determining factor in all such decisions.

Summary

As noted previously, research has shown that journaling can help children in many ways, such as reducing stress, alleviating anxieties, and providing an outlet for feelings of frustration and anger. Further, journaling tends to help improve both behavior and academic performance at school and can help children develop a plan for negative events or situations in their lives. Finally, journaling is one of the most effective ways to encourage communication between broken kids and teachers, and it can be instrumental in helping the teacher reach these kids in a meaningful way. Journaling, perhaps better than any other strategy, gives broken kids a voice—an ability to become an active agent to control their own lives, and that fact alone can be a freeing experience for these students.

For all of these reasons, I'd suggest that virtually all teachers in elementary grades and many teachers in departmentalized schools should implement some type of journaling as a regular, recurring assignment in their classes.

Given the stresses that all children face in today's world, it is imperative that schools help children learn to cope, and journaling is one tool teachers can use in that regard. In short, the benefits far outweigh the time and other concerns, so all elementary and many secondary teachers should be incorporating journaling in their classes.

CHAPTER 7

Triggers and Power Plays

Avoiding Triggers and Behavioral Explosions

Traumatized Kids, Their Triggers, and Power Plays

As discussed in chapter 3, the brains of repeatedly traumatized kids may very well be hard-wired for aggressive behavioral explosions, since traumatizing home environments sometimes become the growth bed for aggression or violence (Perry, 2000, 2014). In their brains, the neural connections made in response to repeated, early trauma ensure that their verbal and physical aggression is the *correct* response any time they perceive any type of threat in their environment. Those violent responses may have helped to protect them in the home environment. Further, traumatized children might perceive virtually anything as a threat that then elicits a verbal or physically violent response. For these children, virtually anything can trigger such a violent explosion (Craig, 2017; Perry, 2000).

The neural connections made by some of these children in early childhood ensure that verbal and physical aggression is the correct response any time they perceive any type of threat in their environment.

In their minds, such a threat might be any ordinary event in the classroom; something like having another student accidently brush their shoulder when they walk by the desk, or having the teacher call on them for an answer that they may not know in a lesson that, up until that moment, had been going smoothly. It may seem that traumatized kids seem to "explode at everything!"—a phrase I've heard from many teachers about many such kids.

When these children are described in this realistic but incomplete fashion, I and most other veteran teachers are forced to ask, "How, by all that is holy, can I possibly teach this child?" These students may seem to be ticking time bombs of rage or verbal aggression (Bender, 2016; Perry, 2014), and defusing these students early in the situation is critical.

When such an emotional or aggressive outburst occurs, the teacher has landed right in the middle of a power struggle with the traumatized child, and when power struggles between teachers and students occur, the student will always win (Albert, 1996; Bender, 2016)! At that point, the student can and will invest everything in the power struggle, whereas the teacher cannot because he or she is limited by professional ethics and also has responsibility for other children in the class.

Please understand that I'm not talking about mild behavioral infractions or disagreements in class (e.g., dealing with a student who refuses to complete an assignment). Rather, I'm talking about serious and potentially dangerous, emotionally charged situations. In such situations, the traumatized student is fully invested in challenging the teacher's authority and may even be cursing and hurling insults (or objects) at the teacher. Should such a student challenge a teacher in class in a verbally violent, enraged way, that student is emotionally caught up in the moment and probably believes he or she is protecting himself or herself, since the neural connections that developed in early childhood have kicked in. In short, the reptilian brain has taken over and self-survival instinct via violence is governing the student's actions (Rosenthal, 2018). The student will say and do anything to "win" in such a situation, and teachers should expect complete noncompliance with anything they say.

Of course, teachers do have the ultimate responsibility for maintaining discipline in the classroom, and while their options are limited, they can use an array of strategies to restore order. For example, teachers can send a student out of the room, perhaps to the principal's office, or call the school resource officer to remove a violent child from class. In those situations, professionals have to ask, "Who won the power struggle? Didn't the student win by avoiding the activity completely?"

Further, engaging in a power struggle with an enraged student can be dangerous for both the out-of-control student and the teacher. Walker (1998) indicated that in 75% of cases in which students physically attack teachers, there is some prelude that involves the escalation of a clear power struggle. Avoiding power plays with students, particularly traumatized students, is therefore not only effective from a disciplinary standpoint; it is also the safe choice for teachers.

In 75% of cases in which students physically attack teachers, there is some prelude that involves the escalation of a clear power struggle.

Thus, one fundamental guideline is simple when teaching traumatized kids: teachers should avoid triggering power struggles with these students at all costs (Bender, 2016; Colvin, Ainge, & Nelson, 1997; Fast, 2018). Preventing the escalation of a power play with a misbehaving student is like avoiding a ticking time bomb, and teachers are well advised to avoid, if at all possible, the explosion of anger or violence in the classroom. Among veteran teachers, this skill is well developed, and they can usually avoid the power struggle in such a way to allow the student some space and maybe even foster the development of a more positive relationship with the troubled student. Numerous authors have indicated over the years that the most effective thing a teacher can do is choose to avoid the triggers as well as any student-caused power plays (Bender, 2016; Fast, 2018; Walker & Sylwester, 1998). Techniques for each are described below.

What Are Triggers?

A "trigger" is any situation or event that consistently initiates a behavioral outburst in children (Bipolar Caregivers, 2018; Fast, 2018; Frank, Gonzalez, & Fagioloni, 2006; Richert, 2018). For example, a teacher may ask a child to answer a question and if the student doesn't know the answer, he or she may react with a behavioral outburst. One child standing near another or touching another may trigger a behavioral problem, and while all students, on occasion are triggered into misbehavior, this phenomenon is particularly frequent among bipolar children, children with certain behavioral disabilities (e.g., oppositional defiant disorder), and traumatized kids.

> *A "trigger" is any situation or event that consistently initiates a behavioral outburst in children.*

In fact, for many traumatized students just about any stimuli whatsoever can be a trigger! Given that reality, presentation of any list of potential triggers may seem meaningless initially. Still a general understanding of the types of events, transitions, or changes that might become triggers can be helpful, since some of these can with judicious planning by the teacher be avoided. Box 7.1 presents a list of potential triggers compiled from a variety of sources (Bipolar Caregivers, 2018; Fast, 2018; Frank et al., 2006; Richert, 2018).

Teachers should consider triggers on a child-by-child basis. Over time, teachers will understand that certain types of events are likely to trigger outbursts from specific children in the class, and at that point, teachers may wish to develop their own list of triggers specifically for the traumatized children and/or others in the class. Once such a list is developed, the teacher may wish to share that list with each child's parent and ask if there are other things the

Box 7.1

Potential Triggers for Traumatized Kids

- Stressful negative or positive life events (e.g., the birth of a sibling, marital problems between parents, ending a relationship with one parent or another, moving to a new house).
- Disruption to sleep patterns (e.g., due to neglect or lack of parental supervision). Decreases in the time the person sleeps can contribute to manic symptoms and/or depression.
- Disruption to sleep routines. A regular structure (e.g., regular children's bedtime waking up times, regular evening activities) can help to maintain sleep patterns and energy levels.
- Too much stimulation from external sources (e.g., excessive classroom noise, clutter on a student's desk, traffic noises outside the school or on the playground, harsh lighting, crowded hallways).
- Too much stimulation from within (e.g., overstimulation from lots of activity; excitement about something at school).
- Overuse of stimulating substances like caffeine (e.g., in coffee or cola) or nicotine (e.g., in cigarettes or nicotine patches).
- Abusing alcohol or illegal drugs can cause the person to have ongoing behavioral outbursts.
- Conflict and stressful interactions with teachers or classmates.
- Excessive media exposure, particularly to news about stressful world events.

parent has noticed that trigger the child. With the list thus completed, the teacher can, if possible, plan lessons to avoid those child-specific triggers.

Best Teaching Practices to Avoid Common Triggers

In addition to specific triggers for particular children, some routine events in school, such as transitions between subjects, unexpected tests, and so forth, seem to trigger many students' misbehaviors. Although some of these are necessary in the school day, others can, at times, be avoided. In fact, avoiding some of the situations or events that trigger aggression, violence, or other behavioral outbursts is the very first key to managing broken kids in the classroom (Hall, Williams, & Hall, 2000; McIntosh, Herman, Stanford, McGraw, & Florence, 2004).

Avoiding common problem areas in one's instruction requires some planning, but it is not particularly difficult. This list of effective teaching practices, collected from a variety of sources, will help teachers avoid many behavioral outbursts in the class (Hall et al., 2000; McIntosh et al., 2004; Salend & Sylvester, 2005; Zuna & McDougall, 2004).

Use Pre-warnings of Transitions

Simply letting students know that a transition of some type is coming can help reduce some behavioral problems (Bender, 2016), so teachers should get into the habit of "pre-warning" kids of coming transitions. In that way, the students who are overly sensitive to change can get mentally prepared first, and are less likely to feel frustration if it takes them a few seconds longer to get through the transition. Here is an example of pre-warning. In preparing for a coming transition, a teacher might pre-warn the class using a statement such as:

> *"We'll be starting our math in about five minutes, once we all finish writing our paragraphs. Sometimes you guys get too loud when we change subjects, so for the next three minutes everything in class has to be said in a whisper! That way, we'll avoid any problems."*

Use Peer Buddies

I suggest that teachers use a peer buddy system that partners students together for some of their work assignments. In many cases, a partner of a student with behavioral issues will assist in curbing misbehavior. This is not a strategy to use for all broken kids because some will not or cannot work well with peer buddies, but teachers should consider this option for most challenging students.

Teach Appropriate Behaviors for Transitions

Many broken kids are amazingly disorganized, and this, like many of their behaviors, may be rooted in dysfunctional neuronal connections in the brain (Perry, 2014). In fact, many of these kids appear disoriented when asked to simply form a line or other simple tasks. Teachers may be left wondering how a student can manage to not understand that simple request. Of course, such behavior may result from other things as well, such as social frustration or isolation (e.g., "I have no friends"). Highly disorganized kids, as well as socially isolated students, may both be paralyzed during the "get in line" process, as they wonder, "Who should I stand next to?" They may end up standing in the middle of the hallway, staring at the line rather than entering into the line, while everyone else lines up nicely along the wall.

To alleviate this problem, teachers should give specific instructions to these children. The teacher might say, "Stacy, I'd like you to be our leader, so please come right to the front of the line and stand close to me. I might need you to help me out."

Use a Calming Voice and Call Students by Name

Often calling students by name, using a soft, easy tone of voice, will help calm them, and this is particularly recommended for traumatized students (Craig, 2017). Here is an example: "Anthony, I can see that you are working hard today, and I just want you to know that I appreciate that! I'm really glad to have you in my class!"

Further, even in intense disciplinary situations, teachers should make a conscious effort to use a calming voice. In fact, this is a calming technique used by police forces worldwide to defuse angry perpetrators because it is so very effective. The brains of all human beings are hardwired neurologically to match those we are talking to in a variety of areas including voice volume, voice tone, emotional intensity, physical stance, and even facial expressions (Bender, 2016). In some intense classroom situations, perhaps a noncompliant student shouting curses at a teacher, the teacher will have a natural inclination to match the voice tone, volume, and emotional intensity of the student, and that will often escalate the situation, resulting in an explosion of violence.

However, teachers in these explosive student-management situations can use this "hard-wired" brain-based behavior to deescalate a potentially explosive student. Instead of adding to the escalation of an emotional, explosive situation, the teacher's use of a calming voice tone and volume can, in effect, "invite" the student to match the teacher on a calmer level without so much emotional intensity. This will take some practice on the part of the teacher, but it is well worth the effort.

Compliment Traumatized Students

Although teachers should always avoid false praise, they should make a habit of complimenting students with behavioral challenges whenever they can, and at least as often as they do other students. This will help establish trust and build a positive relationship, as well as helping to foster improved behavior. As one might imagine, traumatized children have not experienced an overabundance of compliments in their lives, and this simple habit of giving out deserved compliments can help these students feel valued in ways that they may not have experienced previously.

Stand Next to Broken Kids

I suggest that, for each transition in class, the teacher position himself or herself near their broken kids. At times, being within an arm's reach can alleviate any problem. Also, when unexpected events occur, teachers should physically move toward specific students with behavioral problems as quickly as possible.

Offer Choices

Offering choices can empower students who, because of their background, have a hypersensitive need to retain some control over their surroundings. Offering choices may, in fact, prevent class disruption. Here is an example. Teachers frequently develop various versions of the same general assignment in order to differentiate the work for students in the class who may need more of a challenge. Imagine an advanced student who is overly shy and is raised in a foster home. Because of that placement, the teacher might suspect that the child had undergone some childhood trauma, perhaps at their original parent's home. To provide that student a choice, the teacher might say:

> *"Jamie, I usually give you a few more problems than some of the other students because you are really, really fast, but today I'll give you a choice. If you promise that you'll work hard and be willing to help other students after you finish, I'll let you choose either assignment and complete it on the computer. Are you willing to do that, and if so, which assignment would you like to do?"*

Give Singular, Precise Instructions

Broken kids function best when there is little ambiguity in their world. Thus, teachers should get in the habit of giving clear, short, directive commands and using pauses to break up multiple instructions. Rather than stringing three or four different transition tasks together, teachers might say, "Okay. Please put away your math worksheet." The teacher could then wait five or 10 seconds, giving time to complete that task, before saying, "Get out your Social Studies book." The after a pause of five or 10 more seconds, the teacher might say "Turn to page 265." These short, specific instructions help disorganized kids complete the class transitions more smoothly, with less frustration.

Establish Clear Class Routines

Knowing what comes next is essential for almost all students and in particular for traumatized students. In lower and elementary grades, posting a daily schedule on the smart-board can help with transitions and perhaps alleviate some class disruption. The schedule should include, at a minimum, what subjects teachers will teach and when. Because consistency and predictability are crucial for broken kids, the teacher should stick to that schedule if at all possible. Of course, changes in class routine are sometimes necessary and may even enrich the class, but they also may be a trigger for traumatized students or students with oppositional-defiant or bipolar disorder (Bender, 2016).

Avoiding Power Plays with Defusing Techniques

In addition to the avoiding triggers that set off traumatized students, teachers must learn to extract themselves from power plays with students that traumatized children will sometimes set up. Should a student, for seemingly no reason, burst into cursing in the class, that student is essentially daring the teacher to take some disciplinary action. Thus, a power play has been set up, and it is not inaccurate to say that the student, at that moment, is a ticking time bomb, daring the teacher to do something to set off a behavioral explosion!

Students sometimes set up challenges to teacher authority as a means to establish more control over their environment in the classroom.

Unfortunately, that is a situation teachers often find themselves in with broken kids. These students sometimes set up challenges to teacher authority as a means to establish more control over their environment in the classroom, or they may merely wish to avoid whatever subject or assignment they believed was coming next in the class.

In these power struggles, the usual disciplinary contingencies and interventions are not particularly useful (Craig, 2017). Rather, in those power play situations, teachers should seek to escape the power play without triggering the student into a behavioral outburst by using one or more of these defusing techniques discussed below. These have the advantage of extracting both the teacher and the student from the power play, and hopefully avoiding the trigger that might send the student into full behavioral meltdown. Also, managing such situations wisely may even help teachers build a more positive relationship with the student over time. Once teachers avoid the power play, they can deal with the disruption a bit later by talking with the student or perhaps by planning a longer-term behavioral intervention.

I suggest that all teachers become comfortable with several of these defusing techniques, and if the first attempt to calm the student doesn't work, try another! Teachers should be prepared, on a moment's notice, to use these defusing techniques. These ideas come from a variety of sources

(Albert, 1996; Colvin et al., 1997; Walker, 1998; Walker & Sylwester, 1998) and generally allow the teacher to escape power struggles with students and defuse the ticking time bomb of student anger.

Inquire about a Student's Anger

If a student looks angry or upset, the teacher should ask about that anger (Bender, 2016). The teacher might say something like, "I can see that the assignment upsets you. Is it something we can talk about?" Clearly, teachers would rather take a moment and have a brief discussion about the student's concern than have to deal with an anger explosion or other power play in class. Teachers should, however, be cautious with this tactic because it might lead to a lengthy discussion with the student, and class time is always at a premium.

Respect Student's Personal Space

Personal space is the physical space surrounding someone, and all teachers should understand how to use personal space when dealing with explosive kids. In the US, like most westernized countries, personal space extends in an oval shape, about two and a half feet in front of the body, but only six inches to the side and rear. Almost all of us in the US become quite uncomfortable if another person enters that personal space, and we might even feel as if the other person is "invading" our space somehow. There are differences in various cultures (e.g., personal space viewed quite differently in certain Middle Eastern and Asian cultures), but in general getting into personal space of school children in the western world is not recommended.

Because of the sense of threat associated with invasion of personal space, such an invasion can trigger aggression among broken kids. In fact, many traumatized kids actually feel threatened in that situation, because some early childhood trauma for many of these broken kids did involve rape or physical abuse, or other physical molestation—clear invasions of personal space. Thus, the wiring of traumatized kids' brains make aggression a "go-to" response for invasions of personal space (Perry, 2014). For these kids, such an invasion will often trigger aggression or even a physical attack.

Almost all police officers have some training about the use of personal space when apprehending perpetrators and/or other angry individuals. This training empowers them to manage explosive anger in most situations. However, teachers have only rarely received such training, so use of personal space is not something teachers routinely do. Still, teachers should learn to stay out of the personal space of students at all times, unless the student is attempting to harm himself or others.

Like most teachers, before entering the classroom I was not taught to use personal space in disciplinary situations, and that led to a major problem in one particular situation early in my teaching career. In managing the misbehavior of a student—Joanne—during my first year of teaching, I invaded her personal space. She had challenged my authority by shouting that she would not complete an assignment and then cursing at me. Then, she put her head down on her desk.

I felt that my disciplinary authority had been challenged, so I responded with increased volume that she must comply; as I did so, I marched directly toward her across the classroom. I now realize that I had matched her voice volume and tone as I marched into the looming battle!

"Oh yes, you will, Joanne!" I shouted. "Now get that book open and get started!" By the time I'd finished that sentence, I found myself hovering over the front of her desk, and by that point, she was rising to the challenge. I saw vicious anger on her face, and realized she was about to come over the top of the desk at me! It was only then that I backed away a few steps.

My only excuse for such poor management is that I had not been taught about personal space in disciplinary situations. Most teachers are not usually taught about students' personal space, but they should be because such insight can frequently prevent the escalation of violence when dealing with most violent students. Clearly, both moves on my part—matching her decibel level and moving toward her—invaded her personal space, and thus I exacerbated a bad situation.

Today, knowing much more about management of difficult kids, I would do the exact opposite. Rather than move toward her, I would merely look directly at her, which would be a much less aggressive move on my part. Next, I would have sidetracked the power-play escalation by responding in a softer voice, and perhaps by asking her a question about her anger. I might say something like, "Joanne, I can see you are upset, and I'm sorry if I've done something that upset you. Can you help me understand why you're angry?"

In short, had I been taught to use personal space awareness and voice tone in my disciplinary practices, I am confident I would have managed that situation better. As it turned out, Joanne was angry with something said to her before she even entered my class—and I was merely lucky enough to catch the anger! Still, today, I believe I would have defused that explosion. Again, knowing these simple techniques—avoiding triggers and avoiding power plays—will help all teachers manage broken kids much more effectively.

Repeat the Instructions

When a teacher gives instructions and a student challenges them or disrupts class in some other way, one option is to merely repeat the instruction rather than respond directly to the student's challenge. It is very hard to argue with someone who is not addressing the challenge point but is merely saying the same thing over and over again. After two or three repetitions, students might stop making counterarguments, since the teacher is not responding to those anyway. They then will generally, often reluctantly, begin their work.

Teachers should therefore merely repeat the instructions, word for word if possible, in a calm voice two or three times after each challenge. This repetition of instructions, like all disciplinary techniques, will not work all the time, but it will work frequently.

Here is an example: A teacher gives the directions, "Please put your English book away and take out your history text." One student then shouts, "I don't want to do history today!" This challenge holds the potential of becoming a transition disruption in the class, so the teacher responds by moving toward that student a few steps (while avoiding personal space) and repeating the instructions, "I said, please put your English book away and take out your history text." Most of the time, students will persist with yet another verbal challenge such as, "Do we have to?" Again, the teacher should repeat the instructions, "I said, please put your English book away and take out your history text."

This idea often works for one simple reason. It is difficult to argue with someone who is merely repeating themselves. After three or four such gently spoken repetitions, the student will, in most cases, desist in the challenge. At that point, the teacher should then turn, walk away, and begin to assist another student. This will sometimes allow the offending student to calm down a bit. However, teachers should never turn their back on an angry student, and if an explosion occurs, they will need to use another, stronger defusing idea.

Make a Joke

Well-timed humor that is not directed in any way at the student can often defuse a student's anger (Albert, 1996). In the situation involving myself in which a student named Joanne cursed at me, I could have merely backed away and replied, "Well, that's one way to go." That humor, if directed at anyone, would have been directed at my own ability to control my classroom and not at the student's cursing. Still, such a joke may have allowed me to escape an overt power play with Joanne and perhaps continue the lesson with other students.

Of course, this recommendation to use humor should never involve a joke about the student or at the student's expense. Still, a bit of humor, unrelated to the specific noncompliance, can sometimes defuse a behavioral outburst before it happens.

Share Power

I also recommend that teachers be prepared to share power in the classroom, up to a limit, with students. If a student challenges the teacher on an assignment or task, and mentions something else he or she would like to do, the teacher should be in a position, at least some of the time, to negotiate with the student and therefore share power concerning when the student may do the tasks (Colvin et al., 1997). The teacher might say something like, "Okay. Tyrone has suggested that we do something more fun than this math worksheet, so maybe we can do a math game today. Let's form two teams, but you guys have to agree that we'll do this math worksheet tomorrow! Does everyone agree?"

Even this small acknowledgment of the student's power can often improve class climate and might avoid a major explosion for many kids. Again, control over one's environment is a huge issue for broken kids, and some power sharing will work wonders for their overall behavior.

Postpone the Disciplinary Discussion

Finally, postponing a discussion of a student's misbehavior may be an appropriate tactic (Albert, 1996). After a disciplinary issue arises, it is typically advisable to talk with the student, but sometimes postponing that discussion can avoid the "disciplinary debrief" until the student is calmer. If a student is highly emotionally charged or clearly engaged, the teacher might let the student know that he or she wants to discuss the problem at a later time, perhaps at the end of the period. Sometimes, merely knowing that a caring adult is interested can defuse a student's anger or rage.

Action Research: A Case Study of Repeated Instructions

In general, these trigger-avoidance ideas are guidelines for avoiding specific triggers of misbehavior or guidelines for a teacher's immediate response to a power struggle. However, some of these ideas can also be used as targeted interventions. Here is a case study example.

In Mr. Johnson's fifth-grade mathematics class, Mr. Johnson found himself in repeated power struggles with Janice. In many cases, Janice refused to complete work in class, while in others, she stated that she was not doing any homework. In fact, she made that statement exactly when Mr. Johnson was assigning homework. The discussion went like this. He said, "I want you folks to do the three rows of problems at the top of page 289 for homework."

While he is completing this sentence, Janice said, "We shouldn't have any homework tonight. We have a home football game this afternoon!"

Of course, on the face of it, that statement sounded reasonable, at least from a student's perspective. Further, Mr. Johnson responded to the objection by saying, "Okay, guys, get real! Most of you don't even go to the football games." Being a veteran teacher, he knew he had made a mistake as soon as he said it. In effect, he had invited everyone else in the class to protest that they were indeed going to the game! Within a few seconds, no fewer than five other students were stating loudly that they were definitely going to the game!

Later that afternoon, Mr. Johnson reflected on the matter and he realized that he had fallen into Janice's trap. He'd participated in a power struggle. Further, he realized that all too often, he had responded to a student's point in such situations when, in reality, the student was not trying to make a reasonable request but merely trying to avoid work. Mr. Johnson decided he needed to break his habit of responding to such student comments.

For the next three days, Mr. Johnson noted the number of times that Janice objected to work or homework or disrupted the class with any type of power struggle. He then put that baseline data on a chart, as presented in Figure 7.1. As those data show, Janice was initiating a power struggle between three and six times each day.

Mr. Johnson decided on a "repeated instruction" tactic as the intervention for Janice. When she protested an assignment or began any other misbehavior, he would merely repeat the instructions. He began that intervention on the next day and continued it for two weeks, while carefully counting the power struggle challenges from Janice. Each time Janice initiated a disciplinary challenge, Mr. Johnson used a softer voice and repeated the instructions. If she challenged him again, he merely repeated the instructions.

As the intervention data shows, Janice responded fairly quickly to this intervention. It is a fact that few students will continue an argument when the teacher is using a soft voice and merely repeating the same thing over and over again. In this instance, the data show that within five days, the number of power struggle challenges began to decrease. By the end of the second week, Mr. Johnson's repeated instructions intervention had all but eliminated Janice's attempts at having a power struggle with the teacher.

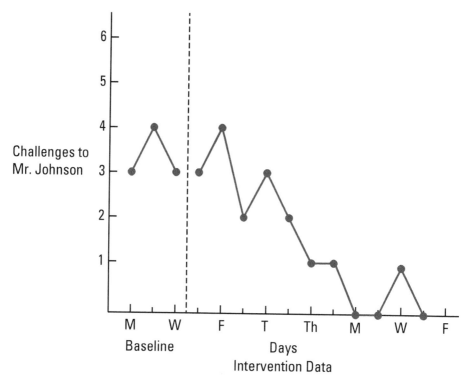

Figure 7.1. Janice's Initiation of Power Struggles.

As one interesting side effect of this intervention, Mr. Johnson noticed that other students also had reduced their verbal challenges to his assignments. In that sense, not only had Mr. Johnson curbed a potential problem with Janice but he had also indirectly improved behavior of several other students as well.

Summary

Avoiding triggers is critical for teachers dealing with traumatized students, and it is strongly recommended not only for these kids but for all students. Knowing what may trigger a behavioral problem and finding creative ways to avoid the triggers is essential in trauma-informed schools. In fact, it is the only way to begin to reach and teach these broken kids.

Likewise, avoiding power plays initiated by these students is critical. As the famous movie quote (from *War Games*) states, "The only way to win is not to play." The same may be said of power plays. Teachers simply have too many responsibilities to waste time in power struggles that can be avoided, so knowing and employing these techniques to avoid them should be considered "survival" skills by teachers dealing with broken kids.

CHAPTER 8

Service Learning for Broken Kids

What Is Service Learning?

An Overview of Service Learning

Implementation of service learning in public schools began in the 1980s and has continued to grow in influence (Cheek, 2016; Furco, 2011; Knapp & Bradley, 2010). By 2008, 68% of principals in one nationwide survey reported some service learning opportunities either at their schools or in partnership with various service learning sites within their communities (Spring, Grimm, & Dietz, 2008). However, the degree of implementation of service learning, the intensity of the service learning experience, and the actual duration of the service learning were shown to vary greatly among schools, and all of these factors can impact the overall success of service learning programs.

Many service learning programs in schools involve weekly hour-long service activities for their students throughout the school year, whereas other schools merely have a "service learning day" once or twice yearly. Clearly, the more intensive the service learning experience and the longer the service learning requirement, the more likely the service learning activity is to show positive effects for the students and for those served. These differences in intensity have created some confusion on the question of efficacy of service learning and suggest the need for a more comprehensive, cleaner definition of the service learning construct.

Although a variety of definitions of service learning exist, I will discuss service learning as an instructional approach that partners curriculum objectives with community needs and facilitates students' hands-on, practical work weekly, over a period of at least six months, as students seek to meet various service needs in the community, focusing on specific projects, either

> *Service learning is an instructional approach that partners curriculum objectives with community needs and facilitates students hands-on, practical work weekly, over a period of at least six months, as they seek to meet needs in the community, focusing on specific projects, either locally or globally.*

locally or globally. This is comparable to most definitions, and while the definitions do vary, most definitions focus on academic content objectives that can be met or partially met through a service project within the community as well as on the time duration for meaningful service.

The concept of service learning was tightened somewhat in 2011, when the National Youth Leadership Council devised standards for service learning programs that include various indicators of high-quality programs. These standards, presented in Box 8.1, specify a number of factors that must be components of high-quality service learning, including the relationship between the service activities and curricular objectives, monitoring of student progress, a requirement for explicit reflection activities on the services provided and their impact as well as stipulation of a duration of service activity that is long enough and intensive enough to meet the goals specified in advance of the service learning activity. With these highly articulated indicators in hand, it is clear that much of what had previously been referred to as "service learning" does not measure up. Thus, for educators who may consider developing a service learning initiative in their school the standards are critical, in that meeting these standards will help ensure that the promised benefits associated with service learning are realized both for the students and for those receiving the services.

Who Is Doing Service Learning?

According to the 2008 survey, 24% of schools in the US have service learning activities for their students, and approximately 4.2 million elementary, middle, and secondary school students had participated by that point in service learning activities (Spring et al., 2008). Those data do show an increase in service learning over previous decades. However, as noted previously, the intensity of the service learning experiences varied greatly, and elementary schools were less likely to report service learning activities than were high schools. In that survey study, 51% of elementary schools indicated that they did arrange some service learning opportunities

> *In 2008, 24% of schools in the US have service learning activities for their students, and approximately 4.2 million elementary, middle, and secondary school students had participated in service learning activities.*

Box 8.1
Standards for High-Quality Service Learning

Meaningful Service—Service learning actively engages participants in meaningful and personally relevant service activities.

Reflection—Service learning incorporates multiple challenging reflection activities that are ongoing and that prompt deep thinking and analysis about oneself and one's relationship to society.

Youth Voice—Service learning provides youth with a strong voice in planning, implementing, and evaluating service learning experiences with guidance from adults.

Progress Monitoring—Service learning engages participants in an ongoing process to assess the quality of implementation and progress toward meeting specified goals and uses results for improvement and sustainability.

Link to Curriculum—Service learning is intentionally used as an instructional strategy to meet learning goals and/or content standards.

Diversity—Service learning promotes understanding of diversity and mutual respect among all participants.

Partnerships—Service learning partnerships are collaborative, mutually beneficial, and address community needs.

Duration and Intensity—Service learning has sufficient duration and intensity to address community needs and meet specified outcomes (National Youth Leadership Council, 2011)

for students, whereas 71% of high schools did so (Spring et al., 2008). Also, schools in low-income areas are less likely than other schools to have service learning activities (Spring et al., 2008), although service learning was being implemented with some success with various underserved populations, such children from low–socio-economic backgrounds and Native American children (Sykes, Pendley, & Deacon, 2017).

At the high school level, data from 2014 document that only Maryland and the District of Columbia included a service learning requirement for high school graduation (Education Commission of the States, 2014). However, the same study reported that 23 states allow for high school credit to be earned via service learning, and six states have passed legislation permitting local school districts to adopt a service learning requirement for graduation (Education Commission of the States, 2014).

Service Learning and Broken Kids

When educators consider the neurological wiring of traumatized kids, the advantages of some type of service learning option becomes apparent. As discussed in chapter 3, several researchers have shown that misbehavior and even overt aggression may be hard-wired brain-based responses to perceived threats among children who were repeatedly exposed to trauma, regardless of whether or not the perceived threat is real (Chemtob, Novaco, Hamada, Gross, & Smith, 1997; Perry, 2000, 2014). Threats against children are occasionally real in the school environment (e.g., bullying, playground violence), but in many cases the threats perceived by traumatized kids are not real. Traumatized kids' brains all too often function based on perceived threats, and even under such perceived threats, the survival instinct based in the reptilian brain becomes dominate. This is when overt aggression and even violence occur, and such aggression or violence is frequently completely out of proportion to the precipitating event because a highly traumatized kid might have perceived a threat where no real threat existed.

However, the plasticity of the human brain holds the possibility of rewiring such aggressive responses of the reptilian brain, moving away from aggression or anger as the go-to response and toward more moderated, reasoned responses. This is accomplished through activities that promote peaceful, thorough reflection on events in the environment which, previously, may have been perceived as threats. In fact, helping others, or any type of altruistic involvement with others, when accomplished in a peaceful manner and coupled with self-reflection on the activity will help re-wire the brain responses over time (Doidge, 2007). Even highly aggressive students who explode into violence daily or weekly can be retrained to show different responses, with repeated opportunities to experience a peaceful, safe helping environment. As these children develop empathy and establish caring, peaceful helping relationships in the service learning experience, they reprogram the neural connections in their brains in more positive ways.

As traumatized children develop empathy and establish caring, peaceful helping relationships in the service learning experience, they reprogram the neural connections in their brains in more positive ways.

Further, having broken kids learn to help others in a caring, structured way, such as service learning, is quite likely to not only reprogram their brains but also to help them develop new and more positive behavioral responses over time. In short, a weekly or biweekly service learning activity in which the traumatized child is caring for someone else or helping someone else can be the very thing the child needs to undo the neural damage from a broken childhood.

Understanding Service Learning

Goals of Service Learning

As envisioned by proponents, service learning is much more than merely structured service within the community. Over the decades, many different proponents of service learning have discussed a wide array of attributes, advantages, and goals for the service learning effort (Cheek, 2016; Furco, 2011; Knapp & Bradley, 2010; Sykes, Pendley, & Deacon, 2017). These range across the spectrum from the development of interpersonal learning or improved behavior or academics through an increased altruistic sense of responsibility for other community members who are less fortunate (Knapp & Bradley, 2010; Meuers, 2016; National Youth Leadership Council, 2011). Many proponents discuss goals, such as improved problem solving and deeper reflective thinking, after students have been exposed to long-term service learning projects. In fact, the range of potential goals is quite wide, as are the observed outcomes of service learning as the research—discussed briefly below—repeatedly shows. Service learning clearly holds the potential for helping students, including deeply traumatized students, in a wide variety of ways.

Of course, academic and behavioral improvement goals need no explanation for educators because these goals are squarely within the focus of almost all educational efforts. In contrast, goals such as improved social engagement and deeper connections with the community are less frequently emphasized in educational interventions. Nevertheless, traumatized kids can benefit greatly from interventions that are proven to increase social connections of this nature, as this entails improvements in interpersonal skills, such as self-sacrificing altruistic behaviors or the development of empathy for others. With service learning activities of sufficient duration, students may even reflectively reevaluate their own personal values through development of a passionate interest in helping others, thus building a deeper sense of connection to others within the community. For broken kids, this can be life-changing.

Investigations of service learning have shown these transformational outcomes for students in service learning programs (Conway, Amel, & Gerwien, 2009; Corporation for National and Community Service, 2007; Meuers, 2016). Service learning depends on and emphasizes a different manner of learning than more traditional classroom activities, and thus these transformations of self are more likely to result from service learning activities compared to traditional instruction. In service learning, students are taught to "serve" others in a meaningful fashion, and in many instances, this will require many traumatized children to change their world view via increased empathy.

The 2005 Youth Volunteering and Civic Engagement Survey (Corporation for National and Community Service, 2007) demonstrated this exact result. The study found that impoverished students in service learning programs became more engaged overall, and their belief in their own ability to make a difference in their community grew. This suggested a positive effect on their sense of resiliency via involved, well-developed service learning activities. At the very least, a new and transformational understanding of the needs of others will help highly traumatized children focus on something other than their own difficulties, and this alone can be life-changing for some.

Types of Service Learning

With these lofty goals in mind, educators must next consider the type of service learning they may wish to offer. Numerous examples of service learning in public schools may be found in the educational literature, but accessible examples may be more easily explored using videos. Educators who are considering implementation of this concept should watch a number of these short service learning videos (Box 8.2 presents several examples) and discuss these with faculty colleagues. As these examples show, there are many differences among the vast array of service learning programs. Still, watching other programs and discussing them together can provide a basis for some of the early decisions on implementation, such as how service learning might fit within the curriculum, what courses might incorporate service learning, or how much time can be committed to service learning activities.

Historically, a variety of different types of activities have been considered service learning opportunities by various public schools. For example, some schools have simply given one or more course credits to high school students for volunteering weekly for several months in a local food back or for similar activities. Other schools have held "service learning days" once or twice a year but award no course credit for these activities, whereas others feature

Box 8.2
Videos on Several Public School Service Learning Projects

I'm Special: Our Service Learning Project (https://www.youtube.com/watch?v=NUPYqZFYExw)

Examples of various middle school projects that connected students with stories of people with differences, and connections to students with disabilities in the school.

Service Learning at Woodbury Middle School (https://www.youtube.com/watch?v=VkrfaL7JgZU)

This video stresses service learning projects to connect students to the community locally and around the world (e.g., making shoes for people in Africa).

Edutopia: Service Learning—Real-Life Applications for Learning (https://www.youtube.com/watch?v=7t30ZMX8uGw)

This video shows student engagement in a greenhouse project to produce food for those in the community. The project used biology students (i.e., every student in the school) to grow salad greens for the school and other schools in the district. Extra impact: students eat more greens!

Learning to Give: Stages of Service Learning (https://www.youtube.com/watch?v=kFd-yiAfrmE)

This video discusses the stages in service learning projects from beginning to brainstorm the project through to the conclusion.

rigorous courses with weekly service learning requirements built in as an integral part of the course. Box 8.3 presents a description of several types of service learning.

Of course, decisions on the when, how, and why of the service activities will depend on many factors. Issues such as school scheduling or the needs of the community partner organization for the service learning come into play when considering the type of service to provide. Still, as the service learning options for a given school are being planned, awareness of the different options above can help educators in the decision-making process.

Box 8.3

Types of Service Learning

Volunteerism—Independent student volunteer work that typically is performed with no pay, and the main beneficiaries are those served. These service learning arrangements have in most cases been established by the students.

Community Service—Services provided to those in the community service site without pay, but with more structure than individual volunteer service learning approach. These options are typically developed by the school district and offered to groups of students, such as a "senior year service learning" option.

Internships—Services specifically provided to beneficiaries in the community that also benefit the students as they gain experience in particular tasks or other measurable benefit from providing the services. These are typically developed by the school because documentation of impact of the internship for the students will usually be necessary.

Field Education—Field education, like internships, is generally more materially beneficial to the student. Field education involves programs that provide students with co-curricular service opportunities that are related or perhaps fully integrated with their formal academic studies. These service learning opportunities are typically developed by the school in conjunction with a community partner organization (e.g., nursing home, animal shelter, church, food bank).

Factors Affecting the Impact of Service Learning

Quality of Service Learning

Educators strive to structure that all learning activities are based on best practices to ensure that they provide the highest quality activities possible, so consideration of best practices for service learning activities in the initial planning stages is critical. Again, the standards published by the National Youth Leadership Council (2011) provide the best guidance for structuring high-quality service learning opportunities. As those standards indicate, the most effective arrangement for service learning is development of a service learning plan in which service learning is organized in relation to specific academic courses within the curriculum as well as the needs of the community-based partner organization. For example, offering service learning in association with a community for the elderly will be different from offering students the opportunity to grow vegetables for distribution to the school cafeteria or the local food bank.

Further, the quality of the community partners providing the placement or setting for the service learning must be considered. A quality partner will take the service learning opportunity seriously and will agree to participate in planning the activity. Further, the partner agency should commit some time and resources to management of the students while they are serving in that setting. Clearly, public school teachers will not be on-site during all service learning activities for all of the students, so a high level of communication between the service learning site and the teacher is critical in ensuring quality learning experiences.

Finally, any courses that include service learning opportunities should have clearly stated learning objectives for students to accomplish, both in class and at the service learning site. These objectives should address real community needs and involve students in both service activities and structured reflection on the service provided, as described below.

Duration of Service Learning

The duration of the service learning project—the actual time that students commit to the services they provide to others—will have a great impact on the efficacy of the project for both the students and for those receiving the services (Mabry, 1998). As noted previously, a service learning day once a year can heighten awareness of issues confronted by various community members and thus can be educational for the students, but such an activity is not likely to affect academic outcomes or social skills of the students, and it will certainly not increase their engagement within the community in any profound sense. These later potential outcomes of service learning are likely to take a time commitment that is considerably longer than one service day.

In terms of the minimum time needed to show any benefits at all among students, Mabry (1998) recommended a time commitment of between 15 and 19 hours in direct service. In school terms, this time commitment is roughly an hour a week for approximately half of the school year, and this time frame is probably the most useful for educators during the planning process. For example, a half-year commitment to a community partner to provide 25 students for service one hour per week involves less risk for a school than a year-long commitment, since once the service learning begins, school personnel may discover that the community partner is not fully committed to the placements or fails to provide supervision as needed. In that case, the school would be free to seek additional or even alternative community partners for the second semester should that become necessary.

Intensity and Goals of Service Learning

The intensity of these service activities must also be considered as a factor affecting efficacy, depending upon the desired outcomes for the students. Intensity of any experience involves more than merely the time committed to the experience. Intensity also includes the depth of emotional involvement students have and perhaps even the empathy they develop for others during the service learning activity. For example, a weekly responsibility to visit with and assist the same elderly person for an hour each week over the course of a year is much more emotionally intense than a group project growing vegetables for the school cafeteria. In this example, the direct contact with an elderly person in need is potentially a more emotionally demanding personal experience than gardening. If one goal of the service learning is to increase both social skills and empathy among students, then an intense experience caring for others is desirable.

With that noted, the gardening option mentioned herein is much more easily integrated into the school curriculum (e.g., in courses such as biology or health), and thus, the academic impact among students of this type of service learning might be more easily demonstrated. In this way, the type and intensity of the service learning experience developed by the school will largely dictate the goals the school faculty might set, as well as the types of positive outcomes that might reasonably be anticipated after implementation of the service learning requirement.

Reflection on the Service Learning Experience

Virtually all of the research on service learning demonstrates that in-depth reflection on the service learning experiences by the students is critical to obtaining the desired outcomes for the experience (Billig, 2011; Celio, Durlak, & Dymnicki, 2011; Conway et al., 2009; Durlak, Weissberg, Dymnicki, Taylor, & Schellinger, 2011; Furco & Root, 2010; Meuers, 2016; Sykes et al., 2017). It is during the reflective process that students develop their insight into the issues represented by the various service sites. For example, assisting disabled veterans through the local Veterans of Foreign Wars chapter once a week as a service learning project is likely to develop a different set of insights and understandings than assisting the elderly. Assisting veterans may help students better understand recent history, whereas assisting the elderly will likely develop empathy for older citizens, as well as insight into how our society deals with older individuals as a sociological issue. In short, the academic insights developed will largely depend on the community partner options utilized for the service learning.

However, most of the actual reflection activities are likely to take place not at the community partner location but at the school. Some class time will be utilized for these reflection activities, and the more integrated they are within the course curriculum, the more likely one is to see academic improvements among the students. A variety of activities can be used for such reflection, such as written assignments, regularly scheduled discussions, or even individual and group media presentations (Spring et al., 2008).

Further, learning occurs best within a repetitive cycle of service activity and reflection on the activity, so teachers should not make the mistake of thinking that a single required "reflective paper" at the end will suffice. Rather, reflection should be ongoing, beginning with the first visit to the community partner site, so activities such as journaling, individual "service learning logs," or even a jointly written "service learning wiki" will result in more and higher quality reflection experiences than a term paper at the end of the experience. In today's classroom, a wiki or class blog would be ideal 21st century teaching tools to make joint socially based reflection an option, and each of these activities exposes all student reflection to other students as well as the teacher, which can be of benefit because students might tend to spend more time on work that will be seen by their peers.

> *Activities such as journaling, individual "service learning logs," or even a jointly written "service learning wiki" will result in more and higher quality reflection experiences than a term paper at the end of the experience.*

Implementation Steps for Service Learning

In considering service learning, proponents state that both the needs and goals of the schools as well as the needs of the community should be considered from the earliest planning discussions onward. Initially, schools should consider their schedule, curricular demands, transportation options (since students will need some type of transportation to one or more service learning sites in the community), and the time commitment to the service activities (Corporation for National and Community Service, 2007; Meuers, 2016; National Youth Leadership Council, 2011). Within those possible constraints, schools must also consider which community partner organizations might provide service learning sites and the needs of those partner organizations. Here are several steps that can help guide educators during the implementation process (Cheek, 2016; Furco, 2011).

Form a Joint Planning Committee

Initially, a planning committee should be formed to develop the service learning requirement and oversee service learning activities during the initial year or two of operation. The planning committee for implementation of service learning at the school level should include all teachers who teach courses that might include a service learning component, such as teachers of biology, history, or health as well as any other teachers who may wish to participate. English teachers, as one example, may be included if the proposed service learning activity involves assisting clients in retirement communities who may have impaired eyesight and may wish to have their personal correspondence read to them. An administrator should be included for discussions involving time commitment to the service learning projects and possible transportation issues.

Many proponents of service learning emphasize student leadership throughout the process (Cheek, 2016; Furco, 2011), so in the early planning stages, schools might invite students to participate in the planning committee. Of course, another option is to include students after the initial outline of the service learning project is developed. The purpose of this joint planning committee will be to oversee the entire service learning effort, not to evaluate specific students' work in service learning sites (that job will be done by the teachers of the courses associated with the service learning requirements). Thus, student involvement at the planning committee level will not result in students gleaning information about other students in service learning locations.

Identification of Potential Community Partners

Agencies within the community are typically used to provide the sites for the service learning options for students. These may include assisted living communities, nursing homes, food banks, community cooperatives, disaster relief agencies, veterans homes, animal shelters, the Salvation Army and other faith-based communities, and many other types of non-profit agencies in which service to the community of one type or another is offered. If faith-based communities or agencies are included in the service learning options, an effort should be made to include agencies of all faiths so that students of all religions (or none) may have an option for service.

Once one or more community partners are identified, those agencies should be invited to have someone sit on the planning committee in order to ensure completely open communication between the school and all involved community partner organizations.

Develop a Statement of Goals, Activities, and Time Commitments

Once the planning committee has taken its final form, a joint planning meeting should be called. For most schoolwide service learning projects, several planning meetings will be required prior to beginning the service learning. During one of the early planning sessions, the committee should develop a set of broad goals for the service learning requirement, and these may include statements such as the number of students participating; the academic, behavioral, or other outcomes desired from the project; or other goals that research suggests may be attained via service learning (Billig, 2011; Mabry, 1998; Sykes et al., 2017).

After a list of goals is developed, a statement should be created on the broad types of activities that students may undertake at the host sites as well as a firm time commitment stating how long and how often students will provide service. The community partner organizations will need this information to determine how many of their clients the students can provide service for and when such service might be scheduled each week.

Inform Parents

Once the broad description of the service learning opportunities and time frames are developed, parents should be notified of the service learning option. In some cases, schools seek permission of the parents prior to offering a service learning course to the students, but in other cases (e.g., instances in which service learning is a requirement for graduation), schools may simply inform the parents of the child's requirement and the location where the service learning work will be completed.

Develop Course-Related Goals, Objectives, and Content Standards

While the planning committee will be primarily responsible for developing the overall plan and goals for service learning as well as identification of the community partner sites for the service, the teachers associated with courses that are involved in the service learning effort will take primary responsibility for listing goals, objectives, and content standards for the service learning. Historically, this specificity of standards and course objectives for service learning has been one point of failure in many service learning programs, simply because no specific objectives were identified for the service learning other than a required number of hours of service. Of course, this is why the guidelines for effective service learning presented in Box 8.1 stipulate development of such course-related objectives. Further, in developing objectives associated with particular courses, the teachers know the curricular content in their respective subject areas and thus should be the primary authority in determining which objectives might be accomplished through the service learning project and which will require other types of in-class learning activities.

Develop Formative Progress Monitoring Tools

Associated with the objectives and content standards within the service learning requirements, each teacher should likewise develop progress monitoring assessments of some type that will help document student progress in the service learning requirement. Again, mere documentation of hours of service is not sufficient for high-quality service learning projects. Various types of assessments will be needed. However, this does not mean only tests. For example, depending on the type of service learning, appropriate progress monitoring tools may include case studies, interviews with those served, surveys of those at the service site, research papers on social issues associated with the service, or group media presentations. Teachers should use their imagination and the input of the students and community service partners to determine what types of assessments might be appropriate.

In addition to various progress monitoring assignments for the students, observations of the student during service learning should be included. Such observations take time, so these will be limited, but both the teachers using service learning and the community partners may be used to observe students and thus provide guidance not only for the service provided but for how the student views the service responsibilities.

Finally, the standards for service learning (in Box 8.1), as well as virtually all of the research on efficacy of service learning (Billig, 2011; Celio et al., 2011; Conway et al., 2009; Furco & Root, 2010; Meuers, 2016), strongly emphasize the critical nature of reflective thought throughout the service learning activities.

The standards for service learning, as well as virtually all of the research on efficacy of service learning, strongly emphasize the critical nature of reflective thought throughout the service learning activities.

Like the progress monitoring planning above, the development of appropriate reflective activities to take place on a regular basis throughout the service learning experience should be developed by the teachers involved. Both individual and group reflective activities should be included, and all types of learning activities can be used to provide high-quality reflection options.

Like almost all kids, broken kids probably benefit most from the reflective assignments associated with service learning, since reflections on the actual service activities are, in all probability, the point at which the students develop empathy, a sense of their own self-efficacy, and a sense of personal control. This truly is the richness of service learning for broken kids. For this reason, self-reports and other reflective activities are great options for these programs.

Set Site Visit Schedule and Begin

At this point, the sites for the service have been identified, parents informed, schedules set, objectives stipulated, and assessments planned and developed. The actual service activities of the students have, at this point, been planned, and thus the service activities should begin. Because these service visits will, of necessity, be tied somewhat to school scheduling, half-year or full-year service visits are typically what schools plan for. However, early in the service, the teachers of the courses associated with service learning will need to hold more in-class discussions and follow-up of the service activities in order to ensure that things are beginning in the right way. After the students have made several visits to the service site, the need for in-class monitoring discussions diminishes to some degree.

Evaluation of the Program

After one or two months of service site visits, the overall planning committee will need to meet once again and begin to monitor progress, not of the individual students but of the program as a whole. General data should be collected relative to how often students visited service learning sites and how often reflective activities were taking place. While individual student issues are primarily the teacher's responsibility, the committee may need to, on occasion, troubleshoot any problems that may have arisen.

At a minimum, the planning committee will need to develop data on the ongoing activities of the program in order to document the successes and failures of the effort. In some extreme circumstances, community partners may need to be reconsidered if the students are not receiving appropriate service learning time.

Proven Outcomes of Service Learning

The number of public schools providing service learning continues to increase for one simple reason: service learning works. Research has consistently shown the efficacy of high-quality service learning in a variety of outcome areas (Billig, 2011; Furco & Root, 2010; Meuers, 2016). Positive effects of service learning include increased academic skills, increased self-concept, increased empathy for others, increased social skills, increased civic engagement, and improved behavior.

Celio and colleagues (2011), as one example, conducted a meta-analytic study of 62 service learning projects involving nearly 12,000 students. Measurable positive benefits were found in a wide variety of areas including positive attitudes toward self, schooling and learning, civil engagement, social skills, and improved academic performance. Students who experienced involved long-term service learning opportunities were better behaved than other students, developed social skills more quickly, demonstrated improved academic scores compared to others, and developed more positive beliefs about their own potential success in life. All of these benefits have likewise been shown in numerous other studies (Conway et al., 2009; Durlak et al., 2011; Meuers, 2016).

Positive effects of service learning include increased academic skills, increased self-concept, increased empathy for others, increased social skills, increased civic engagement, and improved behavior.

Other data suggest that service learning may help with specific high-risk populations. For example, service learning has been shown to help prevent dropouts (Bridgeland, DiIulio, & Wulsin, 2008; Corporation for National and Community Service, 2007) or to help close the achievement gap between minority students and others (Scales & Roehlkepartain, 2005). Research likewise indicates successful implementation with students from lower-income families. Specifically, when children from disadvantaged circumstances participated in school-based service learning, they were more likely to be engaged and believe in their ability to make a difference in their community (Corporation for National and Community Service, 2007). These students from lower-income homes felt more empowered in service learning than in traditional instructional formats (Meuers, 2016), sensing that their contributions in the service venue were important.

As stated previously, this "self-efficacy" factor, or the ability to believe one can have control over and an impact on one's environment, can have a profound impact for broken kids. Traumatized children are often raised in a situation in which they have little, if any, control, so control is a critical motivator. The same is often true for students from economically challenged families, so service learning seems to be an excellent intervention for all such students.

Summary

Service learning is an instructional approach that, while different from traditional instruction, does hold potential to make instruction meaningful for repeatedly traumatized students. The research clearly documents efficacy of service learning when high standards are used in developing the program, the duration and intensity are sufficient to meet the stated program goals, progress monitoring is ongoing, and students are provided multiple ongoing opportunities to reflect on their experiences. Further, this strategy, unlike most others in education, offers the opportunity to fundamentally change students' perceptions of others in society. In a quality service learning experience, students not only develop empathy for others, a trait needed badly by broken kids, but may also acquire a sense of their own self-efficacy in making things better for someone else. In this manner, the participating broken kids gain a sense of control over their own environment, which, as we've discussed several times, is a huge step in their education.

Finally, given the need to transform traumatized students' neural connections in order to bring their behavior more in line with that of other students, this strategy seems particularly appropriate for broken kids. For these reasons, service learning is on strategy that virtually all schools should implement. The time commitment to developing a high-quality service learning project will be more than paid for by the time saved not dealing with behavioral problems of highly traumatized kids, so educators should begin now to implement high-quality service learning wherever possible.

CHAPTER 9
Adult Mentoring for Broken Kids

Adult Mentoring

The Need for Mentors

As one might suspect, broken kids often lack effective and appropriate adult role models in their home. Parents or relatives that are in the home, in many if not most cases, do not display the types of personal skills, interpersonal skills, discipline skills, or caring behaviors that nurture children appropriately. Thus, providing effective role models for broken kids can be one of the most important interventions undertaken at the school level (Gordon, Downey, & Bangert, 2013; Jucovy, Garringer, & MacRae, 2008). For this reason, many schools today address this need through adult mentoring programs (Lawner, Beltz, & Moore, 2013; Vanderwerf, 2014).

Mentoring programs in general were emphasized under the administration of President Clinton in the late 1990s as the nation was seeking appropriate responses to increased school violence and random shootings in schools (Bender, 2007). Since that time, mentoring programs in schools have been used with some success in curbing serious behavior problems and as dropout prevention programs (Adams, 2014; Lawner et al., 2013; Vanderwerf, 2014). Whereas some mentoring programs involve older school students mentoring younger students, others emphasize the use of adult mentors, and both types of mentoring programs seem to work (Lawner et al., 2013). However, traumatized children present many more challenges than do other kids and are likely to respond better when the mentor is more mature, given the lack of effective adult role models mentioned above.

Adult mentoring involves using adults from the local community to partner with troubled students in schoolwide mentoring programs. This concept has been described as a one-to-one relationship between an adult and a younger person who are not relatives and whose relationship is formed to support the younger person during his or her youth (Bender, 2007). Of course, there are many ways in which children can be traumatized, but regardless of the type of childhood trauma to which children might be exposed, research has shown that a caring adult who bonds with a student and is available to the student over time can positively influence the direction of that student's behavior and overall social development (Lawner et al., 2013; Lippman & Schmitz, 2013; Vanderwerf, 2014).

Adult mentoring is development of a one-to-one relationship between and adult and a younger person who are not relatives and whose relationship is formed to support the younger person during his or her youth.

In addition to offering support for kids in crisis, adult mentoring can often provide a basis for sustained self-reflection on behavior as well as on their internal rage, and often this strategy will work with violent, aggressive, and repeatedly traumatized children even when other strategies fail (Vanderwerf, 2014). Further, the body of research on resilience among traumatized children shows that a caring, involved adult can be the single most important factor in promoting more normal social adjustment for these children (Adams, 2014; Lippman & Schmitz, 2013). Clearly, in dealing with broken kids, an adult mentoring program is something that should be considered essential within the school.

A Mentoring Miracle

I was privileged a few years ago, to see a highly effective adult mentoring program in action. Because I was hosting a show on Georgia Public Television on educational innovations at that time, I actually interviewed a number of participating mentors and children in the program in Greene County, Georgia. That elementary and middle school faculty has seen a disturbing trend toward rage and classroom violence and had undertaken a mentoring program by inviting in citizens in the community to "come into our school and change a kid's life!"

The principal, Mr. Willie Miles, is a friend of mine, and he had spoken to a number of civic clubs and churches to find mentors, telling those citizens that there was a great need for effective role models for many troubled kids in their schools and that they could make a positive difference in a single kid's life—and ultimately in the local community. At the first mentoring training meeting two months later, Mr. Miles was expecting 21 people in attendance: adults who had agreed to show up for the training and begin to mentor a child.

However, they were overwhelmed that first evening when over 80 adults stepped into that room to receive the training! Mr. Miles was overjoyed, and the next morning, with so many potential mentors at hand, he said that he had to search his disciplinary referral records to find 60 additional names of kids who could benefit from mentoring. He felt that problem was a wonderful problem to have. Those volunteers, men and women, many retired teachers or other retirees, each stepped up to the call to give back to their community by helping one troubled kid. Willie considered that evening, and that turnout, a miracle, as do I.

Within a year, the entire school faculty was sold on the adult mentoring program. In fact, at Willie's suggestion, each teacher agreed to take one or two additional kids into their class, in order to "spring" a veteran teacher for the morning who agreed to manage that many mentors! Those teachers clearly believed that adult mentoring drastically improved behavior in the school and the overall school climate (Bender, 2007).

Having seen that adult mentoring program work, whenever I speak at a school in which the faculty wish to dramatically change behavior of students, I recommend an adult mentoring program as the option of choice. In short, this strategy can and will change the students' behaviors for the better and ultimately improve the climate of your school (Bender, 2007).

Factors to Consider in Mentoring

Same-Sex/Same-Race Mentoring

Mentoring primarily involves providing an appropriate adult role model to a traumatized student in order for a positive relationship to develop between the mentor and the student, and there are many advantages to such a relationship. However, to increase the likelihood of creating a strong relationship, schools should consider various factors. First, psychologists have traditionally emphasized the critical influence of a same-sex, same-race role model to assist children in becoming successful adults (Bender, 2007). Troubled students seem to bond better with a role model who is "like" them. Therefore, if possible, schools should plan their mentoring efforts around pairing troubled students with mentors of the same sex and race.

While this is not essential, such mentoring is more likely to have a positive impact on the lives of troubled youth. As an example, one national mentoring effort, *100 Black Men of America* (https://100blackmen.org/chapters/), pairs an adult African American male with an African American male student to address the problems of the troubled youth. With that noted, it is often the case that schools find more female than male mentors, so partnering students with mentors of the opposite sex may be necessary. Likewise, same-race mentors may be difficult to find, and mentoring should nevertheless proceed for as many troubled kids as possible.

Mentoring Outside of School

Next, adult mentoring seems to work regardless of the "teaching" that goes on in the relationship. While many mentoring efforts are based around the mentor "tutoring" the student to some degree, the important aspect of mentorship is not instruction or tutoring, but rather building a positive rapport with a troubled student (Bender, 2007). Although many school-based mentorships are initially structured around tutoring the mentee on school work (Vanderwerf, 2014), the most effective mentorships move beyond this "teaching only" dynamic to explore the areas of interest or hobbies of the kids and the mentors. Again, it is not content around which a mentorship is structured, but the intensity of the relationship between the mentor and the student that is most important for troubled, highly traumatized kids.

It is not content around which a mentorship is structured, but the intensity of the relationship between the mentor and the student that is most important for troubled, highly traumatized kids.

Given the importance of the intensity of the relationship, schools must consider what mentoring consists of. For example, most mentoring programs involve adults mentoring kids in school, during school hours, but some mentors may wish to build more involved relationships with their students. Perhaps a mentor wants to take a student to a local football game on Friday evening, or maybe on a church camping trip. This raises the question, what are mentors allowed to do with their mentees? Further, this outside activity issue brings up certain liability concerns for the school.

First, more involved, appropriate relationships can greatly benefit the students as long as mentors do not overstep any obvious boundaries. Thus, the Friday night football game type of outing should be encouraged, with certain provisions. Certainly, schools should get permission from perspective mentors to do a police background check prior to assigning mentors and students together. Also, mentors must obtain permission directly from parents for such activities.

Finally, to address the liability issue in the case of Greene County, Georgia, all parents of mentees were asked to sign a permission form for their children to participate in mentoring. In that form, they were specifically told that

"All mentor activities will take place during school hours and on school property." Further, if the parent chose to allow his or her child to participate in after-school activities with the mentor, those activities were entirely at the parents' discretion and were not to be considered part of the mentoring program.

School Personnel as Mentors

Although this adult mentoring strategy is most frequently implemented when school administrators bring adult mentors from the community into the school, some schools implement adult mentoring on the basis of partnering troubled kids with school personnel. Vanderwerf (2014) describes a successful program in which teachers, school administrators, and others on campus are partnered with challenging youth. Although this strategy can work, the major difficulty here is obvious: there may not be enough mentors and/or enough mentoring time. Schools are welcome to use their faculty as mentors if they wish, but in almost all mentoring programs, the time and availability of mentors is often a concern.

Duration of the Mentorship

The duration of the mentoring experience is another factor to consider. Although mentoring can be effective during half-year mentoring programs, the mentoring is more likely to be effective if it lasts a while (Lawner et al., 2013). Specifically, Lawner and her colleagues showed that programs that adult mentoring programs based on weekly meetings over a full year were more likely to be effective than shorter programs. Further, other research shows that the rapport between mentors and mentees grew stronger among programs that allowed the mentor relationship to continue more than one year (Gordon et al., 2013). Clearly, if a mentor and mentee pair is established for one year, there are many advantages to continuing that same relationship during the next year.

> *The rapport between mentors and mentees grew stronger among programs that allowed the mentor relationship to continue more than one year.*

In the example from Greene County, Georgia, some mentors chose to remain with their selected students for two or even three years. Further, in that example, the mentoring program itself actually "graduated!" Mr. Miles reported that interesting story directly to me when I explored that mentoring effort. After two years of very successful adult mentoring at his school, he got a call from an administrator at the junior high school that his students attended as they progressed through the grades in that county. That principal, pretending irritation, said, "Willie, we don't have a mentoring program, and now I have to start one!" Mr. Miles responded that his mentoring program was working wonderfully at his school, and that his faculty loved the program, but that he was not attempting to force that idea on any other school in the district. Then the other principal said, "No, you're not, but your mentors sure are!"

Apparently, a mentor who had been working with a student for several years went to the junior high one fall and simply asked when she could plan to mentor her student. When told that the junior high did not have a mentoring program, this mentor merely smiled and said, "You do now!" I've always thought that such "graduation" of a mentoring program would be a wonderful problem for schools to have. On a more serious note, this example does indicate the depth of an effective mentor/mentee bond. For highly traumatized kids, this is exactly what they might need.

Mentor Training

Another factor to consider is the training of mentors. Retired teachers, of course, are used to kids and the types of problems they might present, but not all adults are, so some training will be in order. Research shows that programs that provide training and support for mentors seem to work better than programs that offer no training (Lawner et al., 2013), and generally two or three hours of training on at least two evenings is optimal. That time frame will allow schools to undertake a police background check on the perspective mentors and to review school policy on what a mentor should and should not do when a mentee becomes noncompliant. Of course, no mentor should ever consider using corporal punishment, or even any punishment, when mentoring a child, but knowing how the mentor should report problems that may arise during the mentor session will be of benefit. It is also a good idea, during the second or third mentor training session, for the perspective mentees and parents to be invited to meet the mentors.

Administration and Program Structure

Depending on the number of adult mentors entering the school, there may need to be a school teacher or administrator assigned for half a day or perhaps a full day to administer the mentoring program. Mentors will need a contact phone number or email for situations in which they need to miss a day. School faculty should consider who at the school will monitor the scheduling of mentors or the locations for the mentors to work with their students. Without good leadership and coordination, any adult mentoring program is likely to fail, and as more mentors work with more kids, the administrative demands only increase. In the example of Greene County, Georgia, with 80 new people coming into the school to mentor kids each week, someone was needed to coordinate the program. In that case, a teacher was relieved of some teaching responsibilities for a morning each day, and mentors were scheduled to come during that time.

Identification of Goals and Objectives

Program efficacy will be measured based on specific goals and objectives of the program, and in the initial planning stages, educators should consider the desired goals. These goals may range from reducing behavioral problems, to improving mental health, to reducing dropouts. Other issues may suggest program goals such as a higher than average teenage pregnancy rate, high levels of overt aggression, or a need for more respect for others. The concerns of the faculty provide a good place to begin when establishing program goals, and those goals, once identified, will ultimately help plan the mentoring program. Box 9.1 presents some examples of program goals for a mentoring program at a middle school.

Objectives are related to the program goals, but are typically more specific than goals, and will stipulate measurable results for the mentoring program. Box 9.1 presents some specific objectives for a mentoring program.

Which Students Participate?

The number of mentors in many programs is quite limited, and this often dictates the number of students that can be served. However, there is still the question of which students should receive mentoring. Does a particular elementary or secondary grade need intensive help? For example, some high schools might prioritize the incoming ninth grade class for their mentoring efforts rather than eleventh graders or seniors. Another question is whether a special population (e.g., kids with learning or physical disabilities, pregnant teens) needs help. The target population will, to a great extent, determine the number of mentors needed and the role they should play. As an initial guideline, administrators might pair mentors with the 10% to 15% of the kids in their schools who seem to be showing up in the office for disciplinary referrals. For example, an elementary school with 400 students should attempt to identify 40 to 60 mentors for the students who show up daily in the principal's office.

Administrators might initially pair mentors with the 10% to 15% of the kids in their schools who seem to be showing up in the office for disciplinary referrals.

Box 9.1
Goals and Objectives for a Middle School Mentoring Program

Examples of program goals:

- To decrease office referrals for behavior problems
- To decrease in-school (or out-of-school) suspensions
- To decrease the likelihood of aggressive behavior by a student
- To increase the students' attendance
- To increase academic achievement

Examples of specific objectives:

- By the fourth week of the mentor recruitment/training period, 30 volunteer mentors will have been screened and enrolled in the program.
- By the October 1 launch date, all mentor/student pairs will be assigned.
- By the seventh week after October 1, nine out of 10 students will have attended 80% of their meetings with mentors.
- By the ninth week after October 1, eight out of 10 students will have mastered the first vocational skill area assigned (e.g., job application forms).
- By the ninth week after October 1, each mentor will report having at least one in-depth conversation with his student about choosing alternatives to inappropriate behavior in specific situations.
- By the end of the first year, the students will have increased their reading proficiency by at least one grade level.
- By the end of the first year, incidents of aggressive or violent behavior resulting in office disciplinary referrals involving students in the program will have decreased by 50%.

Resources for Mentoring

Mentors at the school will need to know where to take their mentee during a school mentoring session. Thus, optimally, a classroom might be made available for this program, or at least a workspace in the media center or elsewhere. Also, another desirable resource is a teacher who can be in the mentoring room to coordinate the program. Finally, if existing mentor programs can be identified in the district, they can provide a resource for the school faculty; they might visit those school to see how they managed the issues in mentoring.

Of course, funding in any amount will help get a new mentorship program off the ground. Educators may consider Title 1 funds, state grants, PTA/PTO, Kiwanis Club and other community service organizations, and local corporations or corporate foundations. These organizations are also excellent places to seek out appropriate adult mentors for the school. Further, industry in the local area should be consulted since many businesses will offer "release time" for employees to conduct mentoring sessions one hour each week in the schools as a service to their community.

Setting Up a Schoolwide Mentoring Program

A number of sources provide information on mentoring programs (Bender, 2007; Clinton & Miles, 1999; Vanderwerf, 2014), and specific steps to implement a program vary from one program to another. Here are some suggestions to begin.

Select an Advisory Board

An advisory board comprising school staff, mentors, parents, and the administrator should be set up to guide the mentoring program. A smaller group is usually most efficient, but there is a considerable amount of work to do initially. Schools may wish to include others on the advisory board, such as local ministers, business leaders, PTA representatives, and so on, who can help find appropriate adult mentors for the school. These individuals should represent the stakeholders in the project, and their input, particularly for schoolwide or districtwide mentoring programs, is essential.

Identify a Veteran Teacher as Mentoring Coordinator

Generally, I do suggest that a mentoring coordinator be assigned to oversee the day-to-day progress of the program and be available to participants whenever problems occur. Such a mentoring coordinator will help not only to meet program needs but also to increase program stability year to year. Administrators might be used in this role, but as mentioned previously, a veteran teacher may be relieved from instructional responsibilities for some time each day, and that person could coordinate the mentorship program.

The tasks of the mentoring coordinator are many and varied. Working with the advisory committee, the mentoring coordinator is responsible for most of the tasks found in Box 9.2.

Box 9.2

Role Responsibilities of the Mentoring Coordinator

Developing goals and objectives for the program

Identifying, with an administrator, the students for mentoring

Recruiting mentors

Developing guidelines for mentors and using those to train mentors

Providing mentor support, and solving problems as they arise

Matching mentors to students

Collecting data to monitor students' progress and progress of the program as a whole

Scheduling and initiating mentoring activities

Evaluating efficacy of the mentorship program each semester, and providing a written report on students participating, their improved behavior, grades, and so forth

---

Develop General Guidelines for Mentors

The advisory committee and mentor coordinator need to delineate procedures for mentors in some detail. For example, the kind of relationship expected might be described (e.g., at school, or school and community). Box 9.3 presents some examples that help set the parameters of the mentoring experience (Bender, 2007). Any prospective guidelines for the mentoring experience must, of course, be consistent with all school and school board policies.

Identify Initial Mentors and Mentoring Activities

Mentoring programs depend on finding appropriate adult role models to serve as mentors. Visits to discuss the planned mentoring program may be conducted by an administrator, a mentoring coordinator, or other persons at local churches, other religious organizations, and all civic clubs such as the Lions, Elks, Moose, Pilot Clubs, Garden Clubs, and so forth. Obtaining mentors for 15% of a school population is no small matter, but partnering mentors with all children in the school who repeatedly show up in the office on disciplinary referrals will make a difference in the number of such referrals, and that makes the task of finding mentors much less onerous.

Box 9.3

Guidelines for Mentors

Mentors will do the following:

- Undergo a police background check and are expected to relate to their mentees in an appropriate, caring, yet professional manner.
- Schedule a specific day and time each week for their mentoring.
- Call the school on that day to find out if the student is present. If the student is absent, mentors should reschedule their mentoring time when the student returns to school.
- Sign in at the school office when they arrive at school.
- Pick up the student from his or her classroom, checking with the teacher concerning any special events of concern.
- Proceed with the student to the mentoring center classroom, where the mentoring coordinator supervises the mentoring period.
- Mentors may give small gifts on occasion. If there is a time when mentors would like to give the students a special gift (e.g., holiday, birthday), the mentoring coordinator must approve the gift (so as not to result in jealousy among the students).
- Realize that all information such as class test scores, behavior problems, and family structure regarding students is confidential.
- Attend monthly instructional meetings (e.g., all mentors meet on the second Wednesday at 4:30 p.m. in the mentoring center). The mentors will discuss achievements, concerns, or plans. Also, this is where mentors might pick up ideas from other mentors. Ongoing training sessions for new mentors will take place during regular monthly meetings.

Once mentors are identified, and prior to mentor training, the advisory committee and mentoring coordinator should establish some guidelines for mentors on initial activities. Many mentorships begin with simple tutoring of the mentee, and having some recommended materials from the teacher can be a big help to a beginning mentor. However, the most effective mentorships go far beyond tutoring relationships, and the mentor/mentee pairs may express a desire for some activity they can pursue together besides academic tutoring. Such a non-academic activity, or even a joint hobby, often provides the basis for a positive mentoring relationship to grow.

Again, these activities may vary according to the goals of the program. If the primary goal is academic improvement, some form of tutoring is most appropriate as an initial mentoring activity. If reduction of violence or aggressive behavior is the goal, common interest in a particular hobby may provide a non-threatening framework that will allow the mentor to engage the youth in reflective conversations about choices and values. If the relationship takes hold, the importance of the mentor's influence will make a difference in the student's behavior over time.

Evidence of Efficacy in Adult Mentoring

In the modern world, educational innovations must be based on hard data, so teachers should be expected to collect data on how mentees' behavior, social skills, and/or grades may change once they begin a mentoring program. Using these data, the mentoring coordinator will develop periodic reports on the impact of the mentoring program by focusing on the goals and objectives delineated. The reports should include data on improvements in individual student behaviors as well as any specific evidence for program efficacy that teachers provide. Most principals aggregate data on office referrals over a given year, and that information should be compared to the same indicator prior to implementation of the program.

Research on Adult Mentoring

Overall, the available research evidence shows that adult mentoring works (Gordon et al., 2013; Jucovy et al., 2008; Lawner et al., 2013; Vanderwerf, 2014). As one example, in 2013, Lawner and her colleagues evaluated the efficacy research for 19 mentoring programs—programs that targeted a wide variety of outcome variables. These included the following:

Mental health (e.g., depression, anxiety)

Behavior problems (e.g., acting out, delinquency)

Socio-emotional health (e.g., self-concept)

Education (e.g., graduation rate, grades)

Relationships (e.g., with peers or parents)

Risky sex (e.g., early activity, condom use, births)

Substance use (e.g., alcohol, tobacco, drug use)

This review showed that mentoring worked overall for kids of all ages. Further, programs that target at-risk youth seem to have positive impacts more often than those targeting all students, and of course, many broken kids fall into that at-risk category. Of the 19 programs evaluated, 13 had positive results on at least one of the outcome variables listed above (Lawner et al., 2013).

> *Of the 19 programs evaluated, 13 had positive results on at least one outcome variable.*

In that review various mentoring programs focused specifically on one or two sets of goals, and few focused on all of these outcome variables, so the data were analyzed according to the program goals (Lawner et al., 2013). For the 15 mentoring programs that focused on educational goals, 10 showed a positive impact for at least one educational outcome. For programs focused on risky behaviors, seven out of nine worked. Finally, for mentoring programs that focused on social skills and relationships, four out of five worked. Clearly, the specific goals of a mentoring program should be identified in advance of the program since those goals will be used to evaluate the program efficacy.

There were several areas in which mentoring programs showed few or no results. Lawner and her colleagues (2013) reported that only two of the 11 programs that measured mentoring impact on severe behavioral problems (e.g., delinquency, overt aggression) showed positive impact and that no program had a positive impact on risky sexual behavior.

Of course, there are other data that do demonstrate efficacy of mentoring programs in exactly these behavioral areas. Gordon and colleagues (2013), for example, examined the efficacy of mentoring among sixth through ninth grade students and measured social and behavioral outcomes, including unexcused absences, discipline referrals, and "connectedness" with others in the school environment. Positive results were shown on all of these outcome variables.

The "connectedness" variable deserves particular attention when considering help for highly traumatized kids. Connectedness was a concept that stemmed from the research on school violence conducted beginning in the 1990s. That research has shown that in many instances of school violence (e.g., school shootings, fights), the perpetrators are often demonstrably dissociated from any adult or peer at the school. Those perpetrators tend to have few meaningful social relationships; they are rarely members of school clubs and usually do not participate in any extracurricular school activities (Gordon et al., 2013).

This connectedness construct, thus, is clearly critical for highly traumatized children because they likewise show few connections with others and often feel like outsiders. These troubled kids, as discussed in chapters 1 and 2, tend to feel dissociated from virtually everyone and therein lay many of the reasons for their overall unhappiness. Therefore, any intervention that holds the potential to increase their connectedness is certainly an intervention to consider, so again, I recommend that all schools consider implementation of adult mentoring for highly traumatized kids and for other kids in trouble.

Summary

Few schoolwide interventions hold the promise of meeting the needs of broken kids, as well as changing the climate of the entire school, as does adult mentoring. For highly traumatized children, developing a positive relationship with a caring adult can be the most important resilience factor in their lives, and that is why so many schools have undertaken adult mentoring programs. Still, there is a difference between having 10 or 15 mentors enter a school each week and having 80 such mentors partnered with broken kids. Schools that truly wish to address the needs of broken kids need to beat the bushes to come up with the number of mentors that will make a qualitative change in school climate by impacting significant numbers of kids. If educators wish to change the lives of broken kids, as well as implement a strategy that will fundamentally transform their school climate, this is one of the first strategies they should consider.

CHAPTER 10

Restorative Justice

Restorative Justice in Schools

Evolution of Restorative Justice Practices

Restorative justice evolved from practices within the juvenile justice system (Davis, 2014a; Fronius, Persson, Guckenburg, Hurley, & Petrosino, 2016) and is increasingly emphasized in schools as an alternative to suspensions, which were historically used as punishment by many schools. The original concept of restorative justice involved having perpetrators of bad behavior discuss the behavior with the victims to understand the negative impact of the bad behaviors. The goal was to restore a more appropriate, respectful relationship between perpetrators and victims (Davis, 2014; O'Brien, 2014; St. George, 2014). Recently, several agencies including the Advancement Project, the American Federation of Teachers, the National Education Association, and the National Opportunity to Learn Campaign jointly developed a disciplinary toolkit that recommends restorative justice disciplinary practices for schools (O'Brien, 2014).

Restorative justice may be defined as practices and activities that restore students' positive relationships to teachers and others in the school environment (O'Brien, 2014). The idea behind restorative practices is that these disciplinary policies and procedures, rather than simply removing a student from school, will actually help misbehaving students understand the injury they cause and, over time, help build healthy relationships and a sense of community among those in the school in order to prevent conflict and address other wrongdoing (Davis, 2014b; O'Brien, 2014; St. George, 2014).

> *Restorative justice may be defined as practices and activities that restore students' positive relationships to teachers and others in the school environment.*

Box 10.1
Restorative Justice Practices

Victim Explanation. The victim explanation is a restorative justice practice that provides an opportunity for the victim in a conflict to explain how the misbehavior of the wrongdoer harmed him, and the wrongdoer is likewise provided an opportunity to show how he or she will work to resolve the conflict. Such actions may include replacing funds that were stolen, apologies provided to others as needed, or some explanations and corrections that might help restore an individual's reputation if the wrongdoer has been telling lies about a person.

Community Service. Community service is another restorative practice option (O'Brien, 2014). In particular situations, if the wrongdoer cannot "restore" something, he or she may be expected to perform community service around the school or elsewhere to allow the wrongdoer to make a meaningful contribution to the community at large. Such service would have to be planned and supervised.

Restorative Circles. Restorative circles is a conflict resolution technique that schools are using widely today (Davis, 2014a; O'Brien, 2014). These circles involve meeting with the wrongdoers, their parents, and other students and teachers as necessary, and using conflict resolution techniques to reach a mutually acceptable solution to the problem. The circle process is intended to provide a protected discussion in which students, both victims and perpetrators, can open a dialogue with each other. Each is provided an opportunity to speak and listen to one another, allowing both students and educators to offer their own perspectives (Davis, 2014b; O'Brien, 2014). Also, for students known to have some conflict, teachers can use the restorative circle either as a preventative measure to develop relationships and build community among those in the school, or as a targeted response to specific inappropriate behaviors.

Further, restorative justice disciplinary practices are intended to allow students who have violated rules to take responsibility for their behavior while remaining in the school setting. Finally, restorative practices, rather that in or out of school suspensions, are more likely to help address the issues underlying the behavior rather than merely the behavior problem itself. Box 10.1 presents a list and description of several restorative justice practices used in schools (Davis, 2014a; O'Brien, 2014).

Restorative Circles in Schools

Restorative circles are perhaps the most commonly used restorative justice technique in the schools. Sometimes referred to as "talking circles" or "dialogue circles," these circle discussions may involve the entire class to improve class climate or only two students after a conflict has arisen. This is a wonderful technique for highly traumatized kids because the trauma in their background may prevent them from understanding the harm their misbehaviors might do to others. Restorative circles teach conflict avoidance and empathy for others, both of which are typically necessary for highly traumatized children.

There are numerous videos of restorative circles, and reviewing several of these will help get a sense of how restorative circles operate. Box 10.2 presents several good examples. Also for additional information, a book of guidelines on using restorative circles in schools, prepared by the Oakland Unified School District of Oakland, CA, may be found online: http://rjoyoakland .org/wp-content/uploads/OUSDRJOY-Implementation-Guide.pdf

Box 10.2
Video Examples of Restorative Circles

Chicago Public Schools: A Restorative Approach to Discipline
https://www.youtube.com/watch?v=5r1yvyP141U

Edutopia: Using Dialogue Circles to Support Classroom Management
https://www.youtube.com/watch?v=qTr4v0eYigM

Edutopia: Restorative Circles Creating a Safe Environment for Students to Reflect
https://www.youtube.com/watch?v=1-RZYSTJAAo

Restorative Practices Circle
https://www.youtube.com/watch?v=v6ChwR6tzb8

An Administrator's Perspective

Victoria Halferty, M.S. Ed., earned degrees from the University of Georgia, and the University of Scranton in Pennsylvania. She gained certification and taught special and general education (K–12) in three states. I had the honor to teach Ms. Halferty in her undergraduate work, and I have followed her career since. She has taught students with special needs for 13 years and spent the past eight years as an administrator in Reading, Pennsylvania, with both disciplinary and instructional leadership responsibilities. I know her to be an effective professional educator and a no-nonsense disciplinarian with vast experience dealing with some of the toughest students in the schools. She has led the effort in several schools to institute restorative practices and has personally used restorative circles to reduce conflict among students. She is committed to this approach.

After only two days of restorative practices in Bethlehem, Pennsylvania, in 2008, I discovered that what I once recognized as "old-fashioned, just plain talking and listening," is fundamentally effective for managing students with behavioral issues. What a wonderful, though hidden, discovery! The caring, effective listening skills of my family, and in particular of my grandparents—my most admired educators—were linked with my educational experiences by one very simple, fundamental guideline for lifetime learning: genuine conversational skills—reaching toward a common understanding with open listening and thoughtful speaking—is the most valuable factor in rich teaching and effective discipline. To have these conversations with students demonstrating behavioral problems, clearly defined and structured, will build communities supportive of appropriate behavior and learning, a precious goal indeed. After implementing restorative circles within my academic and behavioral practices as an educator, my need for writing referrals to the administration became very limited, as many behavioral problems melted away. My experience as a professional educator and lifelong learner was redefined with regards to my own personal responsibility for truly engaging my students, and developing the art of restorative and meaningful conversations.

Restorative practices return us to an old and effective way of encouraging the human spirit toward growth. People who know they are able to speak honestly, freely, and thoughtfully to others within defined parameters are able to quickly build and develop mutual goals. These practices allow teachers to develop as the "lead" learners in the educational environment, and the students are able to develop as mutually dependent on one another for cooperative, cordial, and positive feedback while building knowledge! As this recognition of mutual learning grows, so does the capacity of the entire learning community.

Restorative practices are not only necessary in the 21st century classroom, they are essential in a time when the digital environment leaves the humanistic world in the past. Without intentional conversations toward behavioral improvement and meaningful learning, our professional efforts to foster appropriate behavior and to direct students toward lifelong learning are futile.

Steps in a Restorative Circle Intervention

As with most of these strategies, different schools implement this process in different ways, and the intended application of this process may determine how schools implement it. Some schools use restorative circles with the entire class, whereas others use them as a disciplinary response to a behavioral outbreak, such as a fight in school or bullying episode. In that application of the restorative circle, this process serves the same disciplinary function as the practice of suspension while having the participants in the altercation actually talk to each other in a structured manner.

Although different schools implement this process somewhat differently, the eight steps presented in Box 10.3 seem to be common to most restorative circle interventions.

Box 10.3
Restorative Circle Steps

Report behavioral incident

Schedule the restorative circle

Initial narrative presentation

Have participants state their
perspectives

Point out areas of agreement/
disagreement

Take responsibility

Discuss alternatives

Sign an agreement

Report of Behavioral Incident

Most restorative circles in schools are held in response to a single disciplinary occurrence, and that event is typically serious in nature. Fighting, having a weapon in school, or bullying may be instances in which teachers would initiate a restorative circle, and if legal issues are involved, the principal must be notified immediately and perhaps even participate. The teacher should document via a short paragraph exactly what he or she saw or what other students reported about the behavioral problem. That narrative, then, becomes the launching point for the circle discussion. A sample narrative of this nature is presented in the case study later in the chapter.

Schedule the Restorative Circle

In most cases, teachers schedule a circle for after school, and the school administrative assistant manages the logistics of scheduling. For serious infractions, it is critical to have all involved students and their parents attend, as well as the teacher and an administrator. Depending on training, some schools have the guidance counselor or a school administrator actually conduct the restorative circle. Others who may be involved include special education teachers, school resource officers, and the school psychologist, as appropriate.

Initial Narrative Presentation

This step and the steps that follow take place during the restorative circle itself. The meeting facilitator—usually a school administrator or guidance counselor with specific training in conflict resolution—begins the meeting by presenting the initial narrative. He or she should present this in a nonjudgmental, statement-of-facts manner, because for parents and others who may not yet know of the behavior problem, this may be the first time they hear any details about a behavioral incident.

Have Participants State Their Perspectives

The main participants in the conflict state their perspectives and add to the narrative. These will frequently disagree with the initial narrative, so the meeting facilitator makes notes on disagreements and points them out to participants. The facilitator gives each of the students in the conflict the opportunity to state her perception of the events without being interrupted by the other participants. If a student and a teacher are in conflict, the facilitator invites both to state their perspectives while taking careful notes.

Although parents of the students in conflict are not required to verbally participate in any steps, the facilitator invites their contribution, beginning with this step and continuing in subsequent steps. In some cases, parents may have critical information to share. For example, they may note that their child has been complaining at home of an ongoing problem with the other person in the conflict. If such information is presented, it should be noted also.

Point Out Areas of Agreement/Disagreement

After both students are heard and parents are presented an opportunity to speak, the meeting facilitator should first point out areas of agreement while mentioning that those agreements may become the initial steps toward restoring a positive relationship.

Next, the disagreements in perspective are discussed. The facilitator might ask one or both of the participants if they understand how the other person may have perceived the conflict differently. In some cases, it might be useful to have participants take the other side of the argument or try to explain why the other person involved might have done what they did or said what they said.

For highly traumatized kids, this step is critical because empathy is an attribute that many such kids do not seem to have in great abundance. The ability to take the perspective of someone else is not a skill that is developed in home environments that include abusive behavior, so this step often represents a steep learning curve for many broken kids. In fact, when restorative circles are used for these troubled kids, it is quite possible that this step alone becomes one of the most important elements in the entire process.

Have Students Take Responsibility

Next, the meeting facilitator asks the participants if they would be willing to take responsibility for how the other party interpreted their actions. In some cases, the facilitator might ask students to apologize to the other party. Again, parents can be critical here in helping motivate students to take responsibility for their actions.

Discuss Alternatives

Next, the meeting facilitator leads a brief brainstorming session to try to find mutually acceptable interaction options that may reduce or eliminate similar conflicts in the future. Options should be listed on paper or the dry-erase board for future discussion. Then the group discusses each option and chooses one or more options.

Sign an Agreement

Finally, the meeting facilitator asks the students in conflict to sign an agreement stating that they will manage any potential conflict in the future using one of the alternatives generated in the previous discussion. The final written agreement thus represents a signed commitment on the part of the students.

A Restorative Circle Case Study

Many districts develop an event form or case study form that delineates the steps above and provides space for the facilitator to write up the various sections of the report. A case study example of this type of report is found in Box 10.4.

Although each of the steps above is not represented by a section on the form, most are. Also, the final part of this report shows that the planned follow-up to the restorative circle meeting is held about 10 days to two weeks after the restorative circle. In this example, the notes show that both of the students have honored their commitments and that no subsequent fights have taken place after the restorative circle. At this point, the principal considers the problem resolved.

Research on Restorative Circles

There is a growing research base for restorative justice when used as disciplinary practices (Fronius et al., 2016; McCold, 2008; Petrosino, Guckenburg, & Fronius, 2012; US Department of Education, 2011). For example, Fronius and his colleagues (2016) reviewed available research on restorative justice in schools and demonstrated that a well-implemented restorative justice program will reduce punitive disciplinary actions and problem behaviors in the schools (Fronius et al., 2016). Several studies in different middle and high schools around the US documented a drop in out-of-school suspensions of more than 80% (Armour, 2013; Davis, 2014).

Further, the longer a student is exposed to restorative justice practices like the restorative circle, the more positive effects in behavior are noted. For example, McCold (2008) reported that recidivism rates changed based on exposure to restorative justice practices with youth who completed the restorative justice program, showing more reduction in behavioral infractions compared to others. Further analysis suggested that participants who completed the restorative justice process demonstrated positive increases in self-esteem and pro-social attitudes.

Box 10.4

Case Study: A Restorative Circle Report

Students Involved: Tracy Sparks, Timothy Attwood   Date of the problem: 9/2/19

Class or Location: Mr. Trotter's Science Class (Second Period)

Date of Restorative Circle: 9/5/19   Problem: Fighting in class

Report of Behavioral Incident: Teacher's Perspective:

On September 2, 2019, at 10:30 p.m., I told the class to get out their science books. A moment later, I looked up and Timothy was standing over Tracy's desk with the science book in the air, and then Timothy brought the book down on Tracy's head. I rushed over there, but by the time I got there Thomas was holding Timothy, backing him away, and Tracy was on the floor with his forehead bleeding. I told Timothy to sit down in an empty desk across the classroom and sent another student to get the principal and school nurse. We wiped Tracy's head with a wet paper towel.

Students' Perspectives:

Timothy: He was looking at me funny, and I heard him call me a queer.

Tracy: Timothy calls me names every day—queer, fag, and slimeball, and he won't stop. He called me a slimeball that day, so I called him an asshole and a queer.

Areas of Agreement/Disagreement:

The students both state that they have never been friends and have no desire to become friends. They "move in different circles." Also, they both see the dangers of spreading rumors around school and using inappropriate names for each other.

Options for Reducing Conflict:

The students decided that it is best to eliminate this problem and that they could do the following:

Just ignore each other

Sit apart from each other in the two classes they have in common

Avoid each other on school campus (lunchroom, commons, library, etc.)

Not call each other names

Not talk about each other, even when the other one is not around

(Continued)

Box 10.4 *Continued*

Commitment: By our signatures below, we agree to behave in the manner we've chosen and do the things listed above in order to eliminate any conflict between us.

Planned Follow-Up: Mr. Trotter and Mr. Alston, the assistant principal, will meet with these two students after school in two weeks as a follow-up to this restorative circle, and again after six weeks. The purpose of these meetings is to review the students' behavior and their ongoing commitment to do the things above that they've agreed to do. Parents will be invited to come as soon as those meetings are scheduled.

First Follow-Up Meeting: On the afternoon of September 18, 2019, Mr. Trotter and Mr. Alston met with Tracy and Timothy. Mr. Alston had the secretary call and invite the parents to the meeting. Mr. Alston noted that he'd not heard of any further conflict between the two students nor had Mr. Trotter reported any. Both of the students affirmed that they had chosen to stay away from each other, and neither reported any ongoing problems. Mr. Trotter said that he hoped that the two young men might become friends one day but that that was up to them. Both reaffirmed their commitment to continue the specific options above to avoid conflict in the future. It was decided to suspend the second follow-up meeting unless the same conflict arose again between these two students.

Other evidence documents the benefits of restorative justice practices in areas other than exclusion from school (Jain, Bassey, Brown, & Kalra, 2014; McMorris, Beckman, Shea, Baumgartner, & Eggert, 2013). For example, McMorris et al. (2013) showed that restorative circle program in Minnesota resulted in reduced self-reported incidents of physical fighting and skipping school among conference participants. Jain and his coworkers (2014) showed reductions of 24% in chronic absenteeism among schools using restorative justice practices.

In a 2014 PBS NewsHour segment, Principal Mathew Willis of Hinkley High School in Colorado indicates that restorative circles have transformed behavior in his high school. Specifically, restorative circles have drastically reduced fighting among students, and he reports a 48% reduction in suspensions based on use of restorative circles. Through use of restorative circles, his students have developed a sense of positive community and were taking more responsibility for their own behavior schoolwide. Like the data in the research review reported above, Hinkley High School has benefitted from implementation of restorative justice practices, and the evidence shows improvements in behavior schoolwide.

Summary

Restorative justice practices are one of several specific innovations promoted by the proponents of trauma-informed schools for two reasons. First, these practices work to reduce disciplinary problems, and second, restorative practices have many benefits that target the specific issues of students exposed to frequent childhood trauma. Cumulatively, these data document the benefits of restorative justice in a variety of ways that are of paramount importance to broken kids, such as reduced fighting, increased empathy, and increased respect among students. Other results show improved self-concept—one component of improving mental health—as well as improvements in social attitudes.

Given these research-documented benefits to restorative justice practices, coupled with the documented numbers of highly traumatized kids in today's schools, it is not remiss to suggest that virtually all schools should undertake implementation of restorative justice circles. In fact, to not implement this set of practices may lead to failure in managing highly broken kids, which, in many schools, make up a significant percentage of the school population. Simply put, educators can no longer avoid responsibility for undertaking restorative justice practices, which are shown to work for highly traumatized kids.

A Conclusion and a Challenge

As I stated in the introduction, my understanding of young adults who are broken, as well as broken kids, has grown rather dramatically in the last few years. Although the education of students with mild or moderate disabilities has been a career-long concern of mine, the extreme examples of deep injury, of brokenness, experienced by kids who are repeatedly traumatized for years is something new to me. I certainly had more than a few of these special needs kids who seemed totally unreachable, and at that time, I didn't recognize the cause or the issues they faced. I'm sure I failed them as a teacher those many years ago. Those individuals represented the extreme end of the behavioral spectrum and I tried merely managing their behaviors, not developing a systematic program to open them up to more normal human contact. Even veterans of the special education classroom, like myself, have much to learn from and about the mindset of those broken kids who demonstrate the most aberrant behaviors.

In short, I've learned a great deal, and I see that I should have been better prepared. Further, I've come to realize that schools need to better prepare themselves for these broken kids as well. Today, schools are just beginning this process—striving desperately to catch up with the fact that these highly traumatized kids are showing up in our classrooms in increasing numbers. The data in chapter 2 suggest that perhaps as many as 10% to 20% of all kids have experienced repeated trauma in one form or another. Although the term "trauma-informed schools" has been around for a few years, few educators took any note of it until the last five years, and only very recently have schools purposefully undertaken steps to prepare faculty schoolwide to address this issue. This fact alone shows how ill-prepared most schools are in dealing with these broken kids.

For all concerned educators, this game of "catch-up" presents a challenge, which I believe is really a moral imperative; we simply must prepare ourselves and our schools for dealing with students who are much more highly traumatized than the majority of kids in schools today. Broken kids who have been repeatedly exposed to highly traumatic situations for years are in our classrooms, and the traditional disciplinary procedures usually will not be effective with these students. We simply must develop and implement more research-proven practices that address the anger, the deep emotional injury, and the control issues shown by broken kids if we are to have any positive impact in their lives at all.

> *We simply must prepare ourselves and our schools for dealing with students who are much more highly traumatized than the majority of kids.*

Thus, I'd like to suggest that this book, specifically the strategies presented herein, must be increasingly implemented, and educators should not see these strategies as simply "another set of ideas to consider." Rather, I'd like to see all schools embrace the concept of becoming trauma informed, and then develop a plan of how to manage these highly traumatized kids, based on facultywide implementation of some of these strategies. Of course, not all schools need to undertake all of these strategies.

To consider on a school-to-school basis what direction to take, I'd suggest that administrators invite a small committee of the faculty to read this book and select two or three strategies that they believe might be most appropriate to their grade levels and their situation. Of course, all teachers could benefit from the information on trauma in chapters 2 and 3, as well as the information on trigger and power play avoidance in chapter 7. However, in addition, I'd suggest that school faculty pick one or two of the other strategies for schoolwide implementation.

For example, implementing both mindfulness and restorative justice practices together should greatly assist schools in dealing with broken kids. Specifically, these two strategies address a number of different issues for broken kids, including helping them achieve peace of mind and increase internal control of emotions and behaviors, as well as ensuring growth of empathy and a better understanding of how others perceive conflict situations. Journaling and adult mentoring likewise make a great pair of strategies, since both open lines of communication that are not currently available in most schools, and such open communication is critical for broken kids, lest they become broken adults. Either we can reach and teach these kids in the schools, or we can finance their living in our jails; it really is that simple. Further, the research suggests that all of these strategies when implemented schoolwide will reduce behavioral problems and improve school climate, and that makes for an improved teaching environment for all.

Thus, the educator's challenge: We must either prepare ourselves better to address the needs of these highly traumatized kids, or we must be willing to "write them off" to their fate, to the hells of their respective trauma, to the many lurid traps posed by the demons of their psyche. No educator worthy of the honor of leading a classroom would ever make that latter choice, so the task before us all is clear: We must help these broken kids.

This is our shared duty, our moral imperative; and for me, this journey of growth, learning, and helping has been one of the most joyous periods of my life. I hope that you can and will ultimately feel the same.

I'll close this book by sharing that joy with you. The letter below presents the ongoing successes of my "Gremlins"—my group of young, badly broken adults. These were victims of addiction, child sexual abuse that lasted years, physical abuse, and neglect, and without exception they are now overcoming their traumatic backgrounds. This letter to them, in reality, presents the hope of success for all highly traumatized kids. It is what I call a "success letter," a summary that I send from time to time to my Gremlins (they have laughingly accepted that term!). You might think of this as closure on chapter 1 and, more important, as the joy every teacher can feel in really, truly reaching broken kids.

Late 2018

Dearest Friends:

Renet and I are so proud of all you guys, and it is time for another update on your successes! I urge you to celebrate every success, and we'll be right there beside you in doing so! You all continue to make wonderful progress, with just an occasional setback or two. Still, you have all rebuilt your lives in major ways, and all of you are succeeding. God is working here with and for each of you, and we see that as we help to celebrate your successes! You'll notice below news on a couple of new Gremlins since the update last April.

__Jason S.__ is living with us now, and we are excited to have another basement dweller! He is doing wonderful things in his life and is succeeding with his Accountability Court requirements, with only one or two hiccups now and then. He just bought a great car several weeks ago, and also just accepted a great new job working in heating and air. He's in my Sunday school class, so most of you guys have probably met him.

__Tina K.__ has enjoyed having her kids back since last April, and in November 2018, she finished the "post placement evaluation" phase with flying colors! The kids are doing well in school, with just a few bumps in the road there. She and the kids attend church with us regularly.

__Ms. Bianca T.__, a Gremlin for only the last five months, just completed her 40-hour GED class. Once she passes her GED test, we'll be helping her to enroll in North Georgia Tech. Very, very proud of this young woman!

__Tammy L.__ is back in college this fall, in her second semester at NGTS. She is in a two-year program in Business Management, and she also took a new management job at O'Reilly's Auto Parts, which she loves! She and her kids will be with us all this Christmas eve!

__Taylor P.__ passed the GED 20 months ago and is now in his third semester at NGTC in web design. He knows computers and already designs websites, so that is the perfect program to give him a great future.

__Samantha T.__ has moved with her kids into her own place and is now working in home health care. She's had a few struggles, but she is working through them and still succeeding. Her son Tyson is playing football this year and plans to play "Santa" at our Christmas party, just like last year—handing out presents to all of you!

__Teresa W.__ has been working for six months to find a more affordable place, and she's succeeded and has moved into a rent-assisted apartment. She is excited to be saving hundreds of dollars each month.

Barbara D. *is a brand new Gremlin, but she has already begun her GED because one of you guys encouraged her to do so! A bit of encouragement goes a long way for folks who may not have had much, and that is a great lesson for us all! Barbara hopes to enter college classes soon, and I hope to help her with that. Still, I do love it when my Gremlins help each other! When you think about it, that's probably the biggest success of all!*

Fredy H. *still works in construction! He is now 30 months clean and sober. He comes to church almost every Sunday, attends meetings, and visits with me at least once a week! I love this guy and admire what he has done in his life.*

Janice F. *enjoyed a wonderful summer as the naturalist at the local state park and is now in her third semester at NGTC in Environmental Tech. She will complete that program in about 18 months. She and Renet knit together at our home at least one evening every week. I think they do that just so they can visit, knit for a while, and pick on me, but who knows?*

Nicki S. *was one of the original Gremlins up "in the balcony" with us three years ago. She moved away for a while but is back now and has been clean and sober for over a year! She's gonna make it!*

Now for a few items of business. Once again this year, we will be holding a Christmas Eve get-together at our home, and all of you and your kids are invited! Please come join us at the house on Christmas Eve about 6 and we'll do singing, read the Christmas story, eat cake and ice cream, and everybody gets a present! If you can, bring along a cake or pie, but don't worry about that—there will be plenty to eat! We'll end at 8:30 or so and head home to wait for Santa!

On a sadder note, my brother and a nephew in NC lost houses in Hurricane Florence late last summer, and I spent time this fall helping them rebuild. I'm still helping them some so I may be out of town if you need me but call anyway. I'll only be gone a few days at a time, and we'll schedule a time for when I return.

Finally, as shown above, many of you have succeeded in reaching your initial goals, and others have just begun. God is working in your lives, and Renet and I are proud to have played a small part in that. Your lives are changing for the better, and the more you attend God in his house, the more he will attend you in yours! You can bank on that. I do, every single day!

Again, great job, folks! We hope and expect to hear great things from all of you. Helping you guys continues to be a joy, a privilege, and the greatest honor of our lives. Please know that we love each of you very, very much.

Renet and William Bender

References

Chapter Two

Adams, J. M., & Dorado, J. (2013). *Schools promoting "trauma-informed" teaching to reach troubled students.* Retrieved from https://edsource.org/2013/schools-focus-on -trauma-informed-to-reach-troubled-students/51619

American Addiction Centers. (2018). *Guide for children of addicted parents.* Retrieved from https://americanaddictioncenters.org/guide-for-children/

Annie E. Casey Foundation. (2018). *Hunger a harsh reality for 14 million children nationwide.* Retrieved from http://www.aecf.org/blog/hunger-a-harsh-reality-for -14-million-children-nationwide/?msclkid=4586344a5e801a46cb776f0d3f8e1f5 a&utm_source=bing&utm_medium=cpc&utm_campaign=AECF%20Site&utm _term=child%20hunger&utm_content=Child%20Hunger

Anxiety and Depression Association of America (ADAA). (2018). *Anxiety and depression in children.* Retrieved from https://adaa.org/living-with-anxiety/children/anxiety -and-depression

Bellum, S. (2012). *Helping children of addicted parents find help.* National Institute on Drug Abuse for Parents. Retrieved from https://teens.drugabuse.gov/blog/post /helping-children-addicted-parents-find-help

Bender, W. N. (2018). *Bible lessons for broken people.* Murrells Inlet, SC: Covenant Books.

Felitti, V., Anda, R. F., Nordenberg, D., Williamson, D. F., Spitz, A. M., Edwards, V., . . . Marks, J. S. (1998). Relationship of childhood abuse and household dysfunction to many of the leading causes of death in adults. *American Journal of Preventive Medicine, 14,* 245–258.

Gorey, K., & Leslie, D. (1997). The prevalence of child sexual abuse: Integrative review adjustment for potential response and measurement biases. *Child Abuse & Neglect, 21*(4):391–398.

Holmes, L. (2017, August 4). Suicide rates for teen boys and girls are climbing. *Huffington Post.* Retrieved from https://www.huffingtonpost.com/entry/suicide -rates-teen-girls_us_59848b64e4b0cb15b1be13f4

Rind, B., Tromovitch, P., & Bauserman, R. (1998). A meta-analytic examination of assumed properties of child sexual abuse using college samples. *Psychological Bulletin, 124*(1):22–53.

Timmen, L., & Cermack, M. D. (1985). *A primer on adult children of alcoholics*. Pompano Beach, FL: Health Communications.

Vazquez, A. (2018, June 8). *Centers for Disease Control: Suicides rates have increased 30 percent since 1999*. Retrieved from https://www.abc15.com/news/region-northeast-valley /scottsdale/centers-for-disease-control-suicides-rates-have-increased-30-percent -since-1999

Whealin, J., & Barnett, E. (2007, May 22). *Child sexual abuse*. Washington, DC: US Department of Veterans Affairs, National Center for Posttraumatic Stress Disorder.

Chapter Three

Adams, J. M. (2014). *New "trauma-informed" approach to behavioral disorders in special education*. Retrieved from https://edsource.org/2014/new-trauma-informed -approach-to-behavioral-disorders-in-special-education/56753

Adams, J. M., & Dorado, J. (2013). *Schools promoting "trauma-informed" teaching to reach troubled students*. Retrieved from https://edsource.org/2013/schools-focus -on-trauma-informed-to-reach-troubled-students/51619

Bender, W. N. (2012). *Differentiating instruction for students with learning disabilities: New best practices for general and special educators*. Thousand Oaks, CA: Corwin Press.

Chemtob, C. M., Novaco, R. W., Hamada, R. S., Gross, D. M., & Smith, G. (1997). Anger regulation deficits in combat-related posttraumatic stress disorder. *Journal of Traumatic Stress, 10*(1), 17–35.

Craig, S. (2005). *Helping traumatized children learn. A report and policy agenda*. Massachusetts Advocates for Children: Trauma and Policy Initiative. Retrieved from https://traumasensitiveschools.org/trauma-and-learning/#student

Craig, S. (2017). *Trauma-informed schools: Specific classroom strategies*. An interview by Melissa Sadin. Retrieved from https://creatingtraumasensitiveschools.org/wp -content/uploads/Susan-Craig-ATN-Interview-Transcript.pdf

Doidge, N. (2007). *The brain that changes itself*. New York, NY: Penguin Books.

Felitti, V., Anda, R. F., Nordenberg, D., Williamson, D. F., Spitz, A. M., Edwards, V., . . . Marks, J. S. (1998). Relationship of childhood abuse and household dysfunction to many of the leading causes of death in adults. *American Journal of Preventive Medicine, 14*, 245–258.

Lippman, L., & Schmitz, H. (2013, October 30). What can schools do to build resilience in their students? Retrieved from https://www.childtrends.org/what-can -schools-do-to-build-resilience-in-their-students

Perry, B. D. (2000). Traumatized children: How childhood trauma influences brain development. *Journal of the California Alliance for the Mentally Ill, 11*(1), 48–51.

Perry, B. D. (2014). *Helping traumatized children: A brief overview for caregivers*. Retrieved from https://childtrauma.org/wp-content/uploads/2014/01/Helping _Traumatized_Children_Caregivers_Perry1.pdf

Rosenthal, M. (2018). *The science behind PTSD symptoms: How trauma changes the brain*. Retrieved from https://psychcentral.com/blog/the-science-behind-ptsd -symptoms-how-trauma-changes-the-brain/

Simmons-Duffin, S. (2018). To teach kids to handle tough emotions, some schools take time out for group therapy. *National Public Radio.* Retrieved from https:// www.npr.org/sections/health-shots/2018/05/23/613465023/for-troubled-kids -some-schools-take-time-out-for-group-therapy

Sousa, D. A. (2009). *How the brain influences behavior: Management strategies for every classroom.* Thousand Oaks, CA: Corwin Press.

Chapter Four

Adams, J. M. (2014). *New "trauma-informed" approach to behavioral disorders in special education.* Retrieved from https://edsource.org/2014/new-trauma-informed -approach-to-behavioral-disorders-in-special-education/56753

Belfield, C., Bowden, B., Klapp, A., Levin, H., Shand, R., & Zander, S. (2015). *The economic value of social emotional learning.* New York: Columbia University. Retrieved from http://blogs.edweek.org/edweek/rulesforengagement/SEL-Revised.pdf

Black, D. S., Milam, J., & Sussman, S. (2009). Sitting-meditation interventions among youth: A review of treatment efficacy. *Pediatrics, 124,* 532–541.

Cooke, M. B., Ford, J., Levine, J., Bourke, C., Newell, L., & Lapidus, G. (2007). The effects of city-wide implementation of 'Second Step' on elementary school students' pro-social and aggressive behaviors. *Journal of Primary Prevention, 28*(2), 93–115.

Craig, S. (2017). *Trauma-informed schools: Specific classroom strategies.* An interview by Melissa Sadin. Retrieved from https://creatingtraumasensitiveschools.org/wp -content/uploads/Susan-Craig-ATN-Interview-Transcript.pdf

Davis, L. C. (2015, August 31). When mindfulness meets the classroom. *The Atlantic* Retrieved from https://www.theatlantic.com/education/archive/2015/08 /mindfulness-education-schools-meditation/402469/

Dodge, K. A., Bierman, K. L., Coie, J. D., Greenberg, M. T., Lochman, J. E., McMahon, R. J., & Pinderhughes, E. E. (2014). Impact of early intervention on psychopathology, crime, and well-being at age 25. *American Journal of Psychiatry, 172*(1), 59–70.

Durlak, J., Weissberg, R. P., Dymnicki, A. B., Taylor, R. D., & Schellinger, K. B. (2011). The impact of enhancing students' social and emotional learning: a meta-analysis of school-based universal interventions (PDF). *Child Development, 82*(1), 405–432.

Espelage, D. L., Low, S., Polanin, J. R., & Brown, E. C. (2013). The impact of a middle school program to reduce aggression, victimization, and sexual violence. *Journal of Adolescent Health, 53*(2), 180–186.

Felitti, V., Anda, R. F., Nordenberg, D., Williamson, D. F., Spitz, A. M., Edwards, V., . . . Marks, J. S. (1998). Relationship of childhood abuse and household dysfunction to many of the leading causes of death in adults. *American Journal of Preventive Medicine, 14,* 245–258.

Goleman, D. (1995). *Emotional intelligence: Why it can matter more than IQ.* New York, NY: Bantam Books.

Jones, S. M., Brown, J. L., & Aber J. L. (2011). Two-year impacts of a universal school-based social-emotional and literacy intervention: An experiment in translational developmental research (PDF). *Child Development, 82*(2), 533–554.

Lippman, L., & Schmitz, H. (2013, October 30). *What can schools do to build resilience in their students?* Retrieved from https://www.childtrends.org/what-can-schools-do -to-build-resilience-in-their-students

Low, S., Cook, C. R., Smolkowski, K., & Buntain-Ricklefs, J. (2015). Promoting social-emotional competence: An evaluation of the elementary version of Second Step. *Journal of School Psychology, 53,* 463–477.

Shriver, T. P., & Bridgeland, J. M. (2015). Social-emotional learning pays off. *Education Week.* Retrieved from https://www.edweek.org/ew/articles/2015/02/26/social-emotional-learning-pays-off.html

Simmons-Duffin, S. (2018). To teach kids to handle tough emotions, some schools take time out for group therapy. *National Public Radio.* Retrieved from https://www.npr.org/sections/health-shots/2018/05/23/613465023/for-troubled-kids-some-schools-take-time-out-for-group-therapy

Sousa, D. A. (2009). *How the brain influences behavior: Management strategies for every classroom.* Thousand Oaks, CA: Corwin Press.

Taylor, R. D., Oberle, E., Durlak, J. A., & Weissberg, R. P. (2017). Promoting positive youth development through school-based social and emotional learning interventions: A meta-analysis of follow-up effects. *Child Development, 88*(4), 1156–1171.

Upshur, C. C., Heyman, M., & Wenz-Gross, M. (2017). Efficacy trial of the Second Step Early Learning (SSEL) curriculum: Preliminary outcomes. *Journal of Applied Developmental Psychology, 50,* 15–25.

Vega, V. (2012/2017). Social and emotional learning research review. *Edutopia.org.* Retrieved from https://www.edutopia.org/sel-research-learning-outcomes

Chapter Five

Albrecht, N. J., Albrecht, P. M., & Cohen, M. (2012). Mindfully teaching in the classroom: A literature review. *Australian Journal of Teacher Education, 37*(12), 1–13.

Campbell, E. (2013, October 30). *Research round-up: Mindfulness in schools.* Retrieved from https://greatergood.berkeley.edu/article/item/research_round_up_school_based_mindfulness_programs

Caprino, K. (2014, February 12). 5 mindfulness steps that guarantee increased success and vitality. *Forbes.* Retrieved from http://www.forbes.com/sites/kathycaprino/2014/02/12/5-mindfulness-steps-that-guarantee-increased-success-and-vitality

Cox, J. (2015). *Classroom management meditation exercises for teachers.* Retrieved from www.teachhub.com/classroom-management-meditation-exercises-teachers

Davis, L. C. (2015, August 31). When mindfulness meets the classroom. *The Atlantic.* Retrieved from https://www.theatlantic.com/education/archive/2015/08/mindfulness-education-schools-meditation/402469/

Fleming, D. C., Ritchie, B., & Fleming, E. R. (1983). Fostering the social adjustment of disturbed students. *Teaching Exceptional Children, 15,* 172–175.

Greenberg, M. T., & Harris, A. R. (2012). Nurturing mindfulness in children and youth: Current state of research. *Child Development Perspectives, 6*(2), 161–166.

Harris, E. A. (2015, October 24). Under stress: Students in New York schools find calm in meditation. *New York Times.* Retrieved from https://www.nytimes.com/2015/10/24/nyregion/under-stress-students-in-new-york-schools-find-calm-in-meditation.html

Klatta, M., Harpsterb, K., Brownea, E., White, S., & Case-Smith, J. (2013). Feasibility and preliminary outcomes for Move-Into-Learning: An arts-based mindfulness classroom intervention. *Journal of Positive Psychology*. Retrieved from https://osuwmcdigital.osu .edu/sitetool/sites/familymedicinepublic/documents/articles/Klatt_article.pdf

Oaklander, M. (2015). Mini-meditators. *Time*. Retrieved from www.michigan.gov /cdocuments/mdcs/wellnessArticle_482372_7.pdf

Robin, A., Schneider, M., & Dolnick, M. (1976). The Turtle Technique: An extended case study of self-control in the classroom. *Psychology in the Schools, 13*, 449–453.

Schneider, M. (1974). Turtle Technique in the classroom. *Teaching Exceptional Children, 7*, 21–24.

Schonert-Reichl, K. A., & Lawlor, M. S. (2010). The effects of a mindfulness-based education program on pre-and early adolescents' well-being and social and emotional competence. *Mindfulness, 1*, 137–151.

Schwartz, K. (2016). *What changes when a school embraces mindfulness?* Retrieved from http://www.kqued.org/mindshift/2016/03/30/what-changes-when-a-school -embraces-mindfulness/

Semple, R. J., Reid, E. F. G., & Miller, L. (2005). Treating anxiety with Mindfulness: An open trial of mindfulness training for anxious children. *Journal of Cognitive Psychotherapy, 19*(4), 379–392.

Sousa, D. A. (2009). *How the brain influences behavior: Management strategies for every classroom*. Thousand Oaks, CA: Corwin Press.

Thomas, L. (2016, February 1). Mindful facilitation: Don't do something, just stand there. *Edutopia.org*. Retrieved from https://www.edutopia.org/blog/mindful-facilitation -pbl-laura-thomas?utm_)source=twitter&utm_medium-socialflow

Welham, H. (2014, July 23). How to introduce mindfulness into your classroom: Nine handy tips. *The Guardian*. Retrieved from https://www.theguardian.com/teacher -network/teacher-blog/2014/jul/23/how-to-mindfulness-classroom-tips

Chapter Six

Adams, K. (2018). *It's easy to write*. Wheat Ridge, CO: Center for Journal Therapy. Retrieved from https://journaltherapy.com/journal-cafe-3/journal-course/

Dunlap, J. C. (2006). Using guided reflective journaling activities to capture students' changing perceptions. *TechTrends, 50*(6), 20–26.

Finley, C. (2010). The importance of student journals and how to respond efficiently. *Edutopia*. Retrieved from https://www.edutopia.org/blog/student-journals-efficient -teacher-responses

Fritson, K. K. (2008). Impact of journaling on students' self-efficacy and locus of control. *InSight: A Journal of Scholarly Teaching, 3*, 75–81.

Greenawald, E. (2018). 8 ways to stop thinking about journaling and actually start journaling. *The Muse*. Retrieved from https://www.themuse.com/advice/8-ways -to-stop-thinking-about-journaling-and-actually-start-journaling

Grothaus, M. (2015). Why journaling is good for your health (and 8 tips to get better). *Fast Company*. Retrieved from https://www.fastcompany.com/3041487/8-tips-to -more-effective-journaling-for-health

Lewis, B. (2017). *Journal writing in the elementary classroom*. Retrieved from https:// www.thoughtco.com/journal-writing-in-the-elementary-classroom-2081069

Murray, B. (2002). Writing to heal. *Monitor on Psychology, 33*(6), 54–62.

O'Connel, T., & Dyment, J. (2006). Reflections on using journals in higher education: A focus group discussion with faculty. *Assessment and Evaluation in Higher Education, 31*(6), 671–691.

Scott, E. (2018). *The benefits of journaling for stress management.* Retrieved from https://www.verywellmind.com/the-benefits-of-journaling-for-stress-management-3144611

Stosny, S. (2013). The good and bad of journaling: Use it as a tool to improve or appreciate. *Psychology Today.* Retrieved from https://www.psychologytoday.com/us/blog/anger-in-the-age-entitlement/201309/the-good-and-the-bad-journaling

Ullrich, P. M., & Lutgendorf, S. K. (2002). Journaling about stressful events: Effects of cognitive processing and emotional expression. *Annals of Behavioral Medicine, 24*(3), 244–250.

University of Rochester Medical Center. (2018). *Journaling for mental health.* https://www.urmc.rochester.edu/encyclopedia/content.aspx?ContentID=4552&ContentTypeID=1

Chapter Seven

Albert, L. (1996). *Cooperative discipline.* Circle Pines, MN: American Guidance Service.

Bender, W. N. (2016). *20 disciplinary strategies for working with challenging students.* West Palm Beach, FL: Learning Sciences International.

Bipolar Caregivers. (2018). *Common bipolar triggers.* Retrieved from https://bipolarcaregivers.org/treatment-and-management/common-bipolar-triggers

Colvin, G., Ainge, D., & Nelson, R. (1997). How to defuse confrontations. *Exceptional Children, 64,* 47–51.

Craig, S. (2017). Trauma-informed schools: Specific classroom strategies. An interview by Melissa Sadin. Retrieved from https://creatingtraumasensitiveschools.org/wp-content/uploads/Susan-Craig-ATN-Interview-Transcript.pdf

Fast, J. (2018). *What are triggers and how do they affect bipolar disorder?* Retrieved from https://www.healthyplace.com/bipolar-disorder/bipolar-treatment/how-triggers-affect-bipolar-disorder-gsd

Frank, E., Gonzalez, J. M., & Fagioloni, A. (2006). The importance of routine for preventing recurrence in bipolar disorder. *American Journal of Psychiatry, 163*(6), 981–985.

Hall, N., Williams, J., & Hall, P. D. (2000). Fresh approaches with oppositional students. *Reclaiming Children and Youth, 8,* 291–236.

McIntosh, K., Herman, K., Stanford, A., McGraw, K., & Florence, K. (2004). Teaching transition: Techniques for promoting success between lessons. *Teaching Exceptional Children, 37,* 26–31.

Perry, B. D. (2000). Traumatized children: How childhood trauma influences brain development. *Journal of the California Alliance for the Mentally Ill, 11*(1), 48–51.

Perry, B. D. (2014). *Helping traumatized children: A brief overview for caregivers.* Retrieved from https://childtrauma.org/wp-content/uploads/2014/01/Helping_Traumatized_Children_Caregivers_Perry1.pdf

Richert, K. (2018). *Managing violent and explosive behavior in young children.* Retrieved from http://teaching.monster.com/benefits/articles/2721-managing-violent-explosive-behavior-in-young-children-

References

Rosenthal, M. (2018). *The science behind PTSD symptoms: How trauma changes the brain.* Retrieved from https://psychcentral.com/blog/the-science-behind-ptsd-symptoms-how-trauma-changes-the-brain/

Salend, S. J., & Sylvester, S. (2005). Understanding and addressing oppositional and defiant class behaviors. *Teaching Exceptional Children, 37,* 32–39.

Walker, H., & Sylwester, B. (1998). Reducing students' refusal and resistance. *Teaching Exceptional Children, 30*(6), 52–58.

Walker, R. (1998). *Discipline without disruption.* A presentation appearing at the Tough Kid Professional Development Teleconference (Bender, W. N., & McLaughlin, P., eds.). Athens, GA: University of Georgia.

Zuna, N., & McDougall, D. (2004). Using positive behavioral support to manage avoidance of academic tasks. *Teaching Exceptional Children, 37,* 19–25.

Chapter Eight

Billig, S. H. (2011). Making the most of your time: Implementing the K–12 service-learning standards for quality practice. *Prevention Researcher, 18*(1), 8–12.

Bridgeland, J. M., DiIulio, J. J., Jr., & Wulsin, S. C. (2008). *Engaged for success: Service-learning as a tool for high school dropout prevention.* Washington, DC: Civic Enterprises.

Celio, C. L., Durlak, J., & Dymnicki, A. (2011). A meta-analysis of the impact of service-learning on students. *Journal of Experiential Education, 34*(2), 164–181.

Cheek, K. (2016). *Six steps for successful service learning.* Retrieved from https://www.plt.org/educator-tips/6-steps-for-successful-service-learning/

Chemtob, C. M., Novaco, R. W., Hamada, R. S., Gross, D. M., & Smith, G. (1997). Anger regulation deficits in combat-related posttraumatic stress disorder. *Journal of Traumatic Stress, 10*(1), 17–35.

Conway, J. M., Amel, E. L., & Gerwien, D. P. (2009). Teaching and learning in the social context: A meta-analysis of service learning's effects on academic, personal, social, and citizenship outcomes. *Teaching of Psychology, 36,* 233–245.

Corporation for National and Community Service. (2007). *Leveling the path to participation: Volunteering and civic engagement among youth from disadvantaged circumstances.* Brief 3 in the Youth Helping America Series. Washington, DC: Author.

Doidge, N. (2007). *The brain that changes itself.* New York, NY: Penguin Books.

Durlak, J. A., Weissberg, R. P., Dymnicki, A. B., Taylor, R. D., & Schellinger, K. B. (2011). The impact of enhancing students' social and emotional learning: A meta-analysis of school-based universal interventions. *Child Development, 82,* 405–432.

Education Commission of the States. (2014). *High school graduation requirement or credit toward graduation: Service-learning/community service.* Retrieved from http://ecs.force.com/mbdata/mbquest3RTE?Rep=SL1301

Furco, A. (2011, October). Service-learning: A balanced approach to experiential education. *The International Journal for Global and Development Education Research,* (0), 71–76. Retrieved from http://educacio-cp89.webjoomla.es/wp-content/uploads/03-Furco-1-English.pdf

Furco, A., & Root, S. (2010). Research demonstrates the value of service learning. *Phi Delta Kappan, 91*(5), 16–20.

Knapp, T. D., & Bradley, J. F. (2010). The effectiveness of service-learning: It's not always what you think. *Journal of Experiential Education, 33*(3), 208–224.

Mabry, J. B. (1998). Pedagogical variations in service-learning and student outcomes. How time, contact, and reflection matter. *Michigan Journal of Community Service Learning, 5*, 32–47.

Meuers, A. (2016). *Service-learning and academic success.* Retrieved from https://nylc .org/2016/07/06/service-learning-academic-success/

National Youth Leadership Council. (2011). *K–12 service-learning standards for quality practice.* Retrieved from http://www.nylc.org/k-12-service-learning-standards -quality-practice

Perry, B. D. (2000). Traumatized children: How childhood trauma influences brain development. *Journal of the California Alliance for the Mentally Ill, 11*(1), 48–51.

Perry, B. D. (2014). *Helping traumatized children: A brief overview for caregivers.* Retrieved from https://childtrauma.org/wp-content/uploads/2014/01/Helping _Traumatized_Children_Caregivers_Perry1.pdf

Scales, P. C., & Roehlkepartain, E. C. (2005). Can service-learning help reduce the achievement gap? New research points toward the potential of service-learning for low-income students. In J. Kielsmeier & M. Neal (Eds.), *Growing to greatness 2005: The state of service-learning in the United States* (pp. 10–22). St. Paul, MN: National Youth Leadership Council.

Spring, K., Grimm, R., & Dietz, N. (2008). *Community service and service-learning in America's schools.* Washington, DC: Corporation for National and Community Service. Retrieved from https://www.nationalservice.gov/pdf/08_1112_lsa_prevalence.pdf

Sykes, B. E., Pendley, J., & Deacon, Z. (2017). Transformative learning, tribal membership, and cultural restoration: A case study of an embedded Native American service-learning project at a research university. *Gateways: International Journal of Community Research and Engagement, 10*, 204–228.

Chapter Nine

Adams, J. M. (2014). *New "trauma-informed" approach to behavioral disorders in special education.* Retrieved from https://edsource.org/2014/new-trauma-informed -approach-to-behavioral-disorders-in-special-education/56753

Bender, W. N. (2007). *Relational discipline: Strategies for in-your-face kids* (2nd ed.). Charlotte, NC: New Age.

Clinton, G., & Miles, W. (1999). Mentoring programs: Fostering resilience in at-risk kids. In W. Bender, G. Clinton, & R. Bender (Eds.), *Violence prevention and reduction in school.* Austin, TX: PRO-ED.

Gordon, J., Downey, J., & Bangert, A. (2013). Effects of a school-based mentoring program on school behavior and measures of adolescent connectedness. *School Community Journal, 23*(2), 227–249.

Jucovy, L., Garringer, M., & MacRae, P. (2008). *The ABCs of school based mentoring: Effective strategies for providing quality youth mentoring in school and communities.* Washington, DC: The Hamilton Fish Institute on School and Community Violence of the US Department of Justice & The National Mentoring Center at Northwest Regional Educational Laboratory.

Lawner, E., Beltz, M., & Moore, K. A. (2013). *What works for mentoring programs: Lessons from experimental evaluations of programs and interventions.* Retrieved from https://www .childtrends.org/publications/what-works-for-mentoring-programs-lesson-from- experimental-evaluations-of-programs-and-interventions

Lippman, L., & Schmitz, H. (2013, October 30). *What can schools do to build resilience in their students?* Retrieved from http://www.childtrends.org/what-can-schools-do-to-build-resilience-in-their-students/

Vanderwerf, L. (2014). Willmar Middle School developing mentoring program that aims to keep students in school. *West Central Tribune.* Retrieved from http://www.wctrib.com/content/willmar-middle-school-developing-mentoring-program-aims-keep-students-school

Chapter Ten

Armour, M. (2013). Ed White Middle School restorative discipline evaluation: Implementation and impact, 2012/2013 sixth grade. Austin, TX: University of Texas, Austin.

Davis, F. E. (2014a). Discipline with dignity: Oakland classrooms try healing instead of punishment. *Reclaiming Children and Youth, 23*(1), 38–41.

Davis, F. E. (2014b). 8 tips for schools interested in restorative justice. *Edutopia.org.* Retrieved from http://www.edutopia.org/blog/restorative-justice-tips-for-schools-fania-davis

Fronius, T., Persson, H., Guckenburg, S., Hurley, N., & Petrosino, A. (2016). Restorative justice in U.S. schools: A research review. *WestEd.org.* Retrieved from https://jprc.wested.org/wp-content/uploads/2016/02/RJ_Literature-Review_20160217.pdf

Jain, S., Bassey, H., Brown, M., & Kalra, P. (2014). *Restorative justice implementation and impacts in Oakland schools* (prepared for the Office of Civil Rights, U.S. Department of Education). Oakland, CA: Oakland Unified School District, Data In Action.

McCold, P. (2008). Evaluation of a restorative milieu: Restorative practices in context. *Sociology of Crime, Law and Deviance, 11,* 99–137.

McMorris, B. J., Beckman, K. J., Shea, G., Baumgartner, J., & Eggert, R. C. (2013). *Applying restorative justice practices to Minneapolis Public Schools students recommended for possible expulsion.* Minneapolis, MN: University of Minnesota.

O'Brien, A. (2014). Inequities in student discipline: What to do about them. *Edutopia.org.* Retrieved from http://www.edutopia.org/blog/inequities-student-discipline-what-to-do-anne-obrien?utm_source=twitter&utm_medium=post&utm_campaign=blog-inequities-discipline

PBS NewsHour. (2014, February 20). *Colorado high school replaces punishment with "talking circles."* Retrieved from https://www.youtube.com/watch?v=g8_94O4ExSA

Petrosino, A., Guckenburg, S., & Fronius, T. (2012). "Policing schools" strategies: A review of the evaluation evidence. *Journal of MultiDisciplinary Evaluation, 8*(17), 80–101. Available from http://survey.ate.wmich.edu/jmde/index.php/jmde_1/article/view/337/335

St. George, D. (2014). Schools get roadmap for improving discipline practices. *The Washington Post.* Retrieved from http://www.washingtonpost.com/local/education/schools-get-roadmap-for-improving-discipline-practices/2014/06/02/da3257c00e8f2-11e3-8f90-73e71f3d637_story.html

US Department of Education. (2011). *Supportive school discipline initiative.* Retrieved from http://www2.ed.gov/policy/gen/guid/school-discipline/appendix-3-overview.pdf

CPSIA information can be obtained
at www.ICGtesting.com
Printed in the USA
FSHW012308110719
59940FS

9 781943 920730